Praise for *Power Speaking*

"**A**chim Nowak is a highly successful speaker in a very tough market; he trains trainers in New York City. It is not an easy task, but he routinely exceeds their expectations. This book will show you how!"
—**Ralph Langevin**, President, Langevin Learning Services

"When Achim Nowak talks, people listen—because he speaks from the heart as well as the mind. Whether you are a novice speaker or a seasoned pro, this beautiful book will have much to say."
—**David Andrusia**, Author of *Brand Yourself* and *The Perfect Pitch*

"Watching Achim as a public speaker is like watching a skilled conductor managing his orchestra. Achim quickly probes his audience to determine the unique strengths, skills, and needs of all participants and then uses this knowledge to maximize the effectiveness of his speech and performance."
—**Sylva Juliano**, Performance Development Manager, GE Consumer Finance

"Achim Nowak is one of the most inspiring speakers I have heard in a very long time. He has a superior ability to read his audience and present material in a way :that keeps everyone completely focused and engaged."
—**Pamela A. King,** Training Manager, Silver Hill Financial LLC

Power Speaking

The Art of the EXCEPTIONAL Public Speaker

ALLWORTH
PRESS
NEW YORK

For Thomas Nowak

08 07 06 05 04   5 4 3 2 1

Published by Allworth Press
An imprint of Allworth Communications, Inc.
10 East 23rd Street, New York, NY 10010

Cover design by Derek Bacchus
Author photograph by David Morgan
Page composition by Sharp Des!gns, Lansing, MI
Typography by Integra Software Services

LIBRARY OF CONGRESS CATALOGING-IN-PUBLICATION DATA
Nowak, Achim.
   Power speaking : the art of the exceptional public speaker : Nowak, Achim.
   ISBN: 1-58115-361-9
      p. cm.
   Includes index.
   1. Public speaking. I. Title.

PN4129.15.N68 2004
808.5'1--dc22
                                        2004012590
Printed in Canada

Contents

Acknowledgments

The creation of this book, and my thoughts on the process of becoming a powerful speaker, have been shaped by the many inspiring individuals who I have met while teaching and exploring the principles of personal transformation. I am indebted to every single one of you!

Very specifically, I wish to express my deep gratitude to:

Sally Fisher—for having faith in me before I did, and giving me the opportunity to do "the real work."

Ralph and Erin Langevin—for running a classy company that truly honors the mystery and humanity of the adult audience.

Carol Morton—for showing me how to lead with quiet grace.

Twila Thompson, Gifford Booth, and Allen Schoer—for reminding me that without creativity, we have nothing.

Lynda Zimmerman, Jim Mirrione, Chris Vine, Mitalene Fletcher, Alexandra Lopez and all of my friends at the Creative Arts Team and the Kaplan Center for Educational Drama—for providing me with a creative home for all these years.

My many fellow seminar leaders—especially Alisa Alexander, Maura Beatty, Judy Bell, Olga Botcharova, Tim Brock, Herminio Hernandez, Lynne Hurdle-Price, Scott Leta, Marylyn McCormack de Castro, Mike Miles, Linda Carole Pierce, Jose Rego, Martin Roundy, and Denise Shanklin—for teaching me by example and making it look so very easy.

My colleagues in the TAI speaker development group—Robert Anderson, Sandra Carey, Dawn Denvir, John Griffith, Elise Hedblom, Gary Lyons, Kathryn Mayer, Diane Nersesian, Graeme Thompson, and Judy Woodard—for so joyously exploring the boundaries of the coaching life.

Sam Carter—for his wickedly creative mind, and his contribution to *Power Speaking.*

Ellen MacDonald—for her unwavering friendship, and her contribution to *Power Speaking.*

Clare Maxwell—for selflessly sharing her movement wisdom.

Andi Shiraz—for her impeccable insights during the inception of this book.

Dan Diggles and Michael Loman—for connecting me with the right people at the right time.

All of the folks at Allworth Press—especially Tad Allworth, Nicole Potter, Derek Bacchus, and Birte Pampel—for their easygoing approach to the serious business of bookmaking.

And two of the very early teachers in my theater career—Joy McLean Bosfield and Anthony Abeson—for showing me, once and for all, that the body is the portal to our hearts and souls.

Introduction

Let's talk about power speaking.

Sometimes we're fortunate to find a teacher who makes a difference, someone who is able to shape us in a way that transforms what we do for the rest of our lives. Joy McLean Bosfield was that teacher in my life. Back in the late seventies, when I was an aspiring actor in the theater world of Washington, D.C., I was referred to Joy to help develop my voice. Once a week I climbed onto my beat-up old bicycle and huffed and puffed my way up 16th Street, to the slender townhouse where Joy coached her students. Joy hailed from the original cast of *Porgy and Bess*. While I was barely into my twenties, Joy had long settled into her golden years. For a year, once a week, every week, she stood behind the piano in the little room at the top of the stairs, and we practiced scales.

I was not a very good student. Timid, impatient. But Joy always smiled benignly at me, her body draped in one of the angora sweaters she so loved, her hair pulled tight into a chignon. Only when I—yet again—could not reach a note, did her eyes betray a glint of exasperation. And then, inevitably, Joy would turn to me and demand:

"Breathe from your penis."

It's what I did for a year with Joy: I learned to breathe from my penis.

I didn't at all "get" what Joy was doing at the time. But about eight months or so after I stopped studying with her I had an epiphany. It was one of those moments when you're there, right inside the moment, and then all at once you step out of it and observe what's going on. I was in the midst of a rehearsal for a play, and suddenly I heard the sound of my voice as I was speaking. I listened to myself, and I was startled. My voice no longer sounded as I had remembered it. It had a new depth, a weight, a raspy resonance I had never heard before.

"Breathe from your penis."

Joy had entirely changed the way I speak. But more importantly, Joy had planted deep within me the seeds of speaking with power. The strength of our voice is critical to how others hear us, but Joy's coaching reached well beyond vocal technique, down to the very heart and soul from which all speaking emanates. Her message was unmistakable: Be expansive. Say it from the gut. Speak with conviction and passion. Send it from deep within you, all of it.

How we find our voice, and how we find that way of speaking, is a significant part of this book. It is, indeed, the starting point of *Power Speaking*. But it's only one leg of our speaking journey. Let me clarify.

It is now early June of 1998, and I'm standing in the Quebec meeting room of the Lord Elgin Hotel in Ottawa, Canada, conducting one of my public-speaking seminars for corporate trainers. As I coach this group, I witness some of the telltale signs of the novice speaker—the jittery and unnecessary body movements, the fearful gestures, the nervous glances that avoid the audience, the voice that doesn't quite fill the room.

I also notice one presenter who doesn't exhibit any of these traits. Jane is a no-nonsense, go-for-it kind of speaker who presents with a reckless energy. She gestures freely, makes aggressive eye contact, and she works the room. I wonder, for a moment, why Jane is in this seminar; she has clearly been coached before. But as I watch her deliver presentation after presentation during this three-day class, I notice something else. Jane does everything right, but she is not connecting with her group. She is not "coming across." Worse yet, as I watch the audience's reaction, it's quite clear that they just plain don't like her.

I have coached many speakers like Jane—the speakers who have mastered the basic tools of public speaking, and have, indeed, mastered them well. But unless the tools are integrated with a clear sense of who we are and what we project to the world, they will remain exactly what they are: an empty set of tricks.

Power Speaking is subtitled *The Art of the Exceptional Public Speaker*. The art, quite simply, is the way in which we merge those tools with the essence of who we are. I don't mean to sound overly mystical as I commit these words to paper. The truth of this sentence is revealed to me, again and again, as I listen to people speak. An audience will be dazzled by the tricks and the "shtick." For a while, anyway. But what it responds to, in the end, is never what we say or do. It is the personal essence that we convey.

As your coach in *Power Speaking*, I want to take you on the journey toward becoming a true power speaker. The sort of speaker who, yes, has mastered the basic skills, but whose presentation, at the same time, transcends a mere hit list of tricks. The kind whose very presence is able to reach and galvanize an audience. The one the audience will remember. Always.

Does this sound daunting? I hope not. You will become a power speaker by following a clear, step-by-step approach that will help transform the way you speak in public. I have organized this book in a simple, three-part format. I will guide you from a practice of the essential skills to the incorporation of tools that can help you connect with any audience. Finally, and most importantly, I will encourage you to assess and clarify what you truly project, every time you speak in front of people.

In part I—The Art of the Craft—we will focus on the vital skills of the presenter: the use of the voice, body movement, gestures, eye contact, and personal energy. Without a mastery of these tools we operate with a set of barriers, and the audience focuses on the barriers rather than the message we seek to convey.

Part II—The Art of the Connection—explores our ability to deeply engage and connect with the audience. We will look at ways of using clear intentions to help create our desired impact. We will explore the use of strong frames, stories, and humor to compellingly shape our content. We will develop a "dialogue mindset" that involves the use of probing questions and intent listening. And we will look at ways to transform audience resistance. A mastery of these skills marks the difference between a beginning and an advanced public speaker. Your consistent integration of the tools in this section will instantly set you apart from the pack.

In part III—The Art of the Flow—I challenge you to take an honest look at how you come across. It's the work that my colleague Jane never quite got around to doing. In this section we ask some of the tough questions: What are the personal values that drive you as you speak? Where is fear blocking you from "breaking through" to your audience?

How spontaneous are you in front of a group? What would it mean for you to be a more expansive speaker? Your unflinching willingness to examine these questions, coupled with the ability to shift, adapt, and develop, will be your secret to success. It will lift you into the realm of the power speakers who are able to transport their audiences into magical states of flow.

These three parts of *Power Speaking* are accompanied by an appendix in which I offer you tips for the fluid integration of visuals. Each chapter in *Power Speaking* includes anecdotes from my coaching experience to help illustrate, in a very real-life way, the importance of each skill. I will share success stories to inspire you, and I will describe the dynamics of a skill and offer tips for mastering that skill. More importantly, each chapter closes with several well-proven practice exercises that you can readily follow on your own to develop the skills we discuss in *Power Speaking*.

Let me tell you about myself for a moment. When I thumb through a book like *Power Speaking*, with its collection of practice exercises, I immediately want to skip the exercise portion and jump ahead to the next chapter. Because I'm smart and I "get" the concepts quickly. Right? Well, it doesn't quite work that way when it comes to public speaking. There is no way we can think our way through the skills. Power speaking has nothing to do with how smart we are. We change and evolve only through a rigorous application of the exercises. Consistent practice. Repetition. More practice.

Here is a case in point: When I was seventeen years old, a year after I had arrived in this country from Germany, I decided that I wanted to work as an actor. Problem was, I had a rather discernible German accent, and I knew from watching American TV shows like *Hogan's Heroes* that this would be my lot: I would play Nazis. So, every Saturday afternoon, I met with Barbara, my diction coach, for an hour-long session in the lobby of the Washington Theatre Club, painstakingly learning a different way of placing my tongue in relation to my teeth, sound by sound eradicating the echoes of one language so I could work in another. The point, I trust, is clear. Barbara, my coach, did not need to do the exercises. I did. My muscles needed to practice. My brain needed to learn to send new messages to my tongue. My tongue needed to remember its new placement in relation to my teeth, until this placement became the only and effortless way of enunciating. A year and a half later I began to sound American, and was cast in American parts.

Power Speaking is here to offer you tangible tools, instill confidence, and help you sparkle in front of any group. I have repeatedly mentioned the benefits of working hands-on with a coach. This book, however, has been designed so you will not need a coach. *Power Speaking* serves as your personal guide and mentor, and the exercises are designed to help you progress rapidly on your own. I invite you to peruse the book. Jump around. Find your favorite sections, and re-read them if you wish. But then, kindly settle down and start at the beginning. Enjoy the process of exploring the tools in each chapter. And know that, exercise by exercise, you will be well on your way to becoming an exceptional speaker.

This I promise you: the results will astound and delight you. You will experience an entirely new way of "being" in front of a group. You will discover a fearless way of speaking in public. You will be amazed by the responses you suddenly elicit from your audience. But more importantly, you will know the joy of speaking with true inner power, a power that was just waiting to be unleashed!

The Art of the Craft

PART I

One afternoon in the fall of 1989, I happened to pass my friend Mitch on the street. He pulled a cassette tape out of his knapsack. "Go and listen to this woman," he said with enthusiasm. "She's really good." That evening I slid the tape into my cassette player. The woman—as far as I could tell—was a metaphysical speaker. The tape was simple, homemade, with a scratchy background sound that was unpleasant to the ear. What really annoyed me, however, was the sound of the speaker's voice: she spoke in a high, shrill pitch. She raced through her sentences as if she couldn't wait to get to the end. When she finally paused she produced sharp, heavy breaths as if she were gulping for air. Then her fast, high-pitched delivery resumed without variation.

After barely thirty seconds I turned off the tape, irritated by this unsavory voice, and more than a little peeved with my friend for suggesting I listen to it in the first place.

Almost exactly one year after this chance meeting, Mitch took me to a small social gathering in an apartment on West 15th Street in Manhattan. There was a featured speaker at the soiree who sat perched on an ottoman and addressed the group of twenty or so guests. She was vivacious, with a rapid-fire delivery style that was accentuated by lively and effusive gestures. It wasn't long before I realized that—yes—this was the woman whose audiotape I had found so irritating a year earlier. I marveled with a mixture of awe and disbelief at her seemingly endless reservoir of energy. Seeing her in person, I recognized the appeal of this energy. Her voice, however, still had the shrill edge I found unpleasing. And the gestures and sentences moved too fast, as if she were unleashing a flood of kinesthetic impulses that she could not contain.

Sometime in May of 1991 I went to an event at Town Hall, a large concert hall in the heart of Manhattan's Broadway theater district. The featured speaker—yes, you guessed it—was this very same woman. When she walked onto the stage, in front of an audience of fifteen hundred people, I witnessed what fell nothing short of a public speaking transformation. Her voice had settled into a lower, more pleasing range. Her delivery style had slowed. Her infectious natural energy was steady and focused. I was entranced. Instead of observing this speaker's communication blockers, I was able to focus on her message. Instead of getting in the way of this message, her basic communication tools—her voice, body movement, gestures, eye contact, and personal energy—acted in beautiful synergy to support her message.

The speaker was Marianne Williamson, a highly successful motivational speaker and the author of numerous *New York Times* bestselling books. I heard her at a time when she was just beginning to make her mark in public, and like many beginning speakers, she was clearly grappling with how to effectively communicate with her audience. By the time Marianne spoke at Town Hall, she had begun to master the basics that we will explore in the first part of this book.

As I listened to Marianne that evening, I had one of my personal lightbulb moments: Marianne Williamson was saying the very things she had said on that rushed audiotape and at the private gathering I had attended. Marianne had always had her message. Her content had not changed—she had simply fine-tuned her basic communication instruments and had become a true channel for her message.

She had learned to get out of her own way.

In part I, we will have the opportunity to look at what *you* can do to get out of your own way. Chances are Marianne Williamson did not do this on her own. Someone worked with her on the use of eye contact, body movement, gestures, energy, and the quality of her voice. Most public speakers—newscasters, politicians, and high-level business leaders—have been coached on all of these skills. Many have been coached so aggressively that it is difficult to detect a spark of sincerity or spontaneity in their speaking style. Their every statement and movement looks phony and calculated. I call it the Dan Rather School of Public Speaking: stiff, stagy, and entirely studied. Each gesture and each glance draws attention to itself. Each phrase and each pause looks like the tidy execution of a coaching tip that has not been assimilated.

This is most certainly not what we want. Everything we explore in this section is intended to move us away from such a meticulously studied approach. As we become fluid with the use of our basic vocabulary (our voice, gestures, body movement, eye contact, and personal energy) it will cease to draw attention to itself. It will become submerged in how we express the essence of who we are. It will be placed in the invisible service of the message we seek to convey to our audience. Fully integrated, this vocabulary has the potential to transform us into truly brilliant speakers.

CHAPTER 1

Voice

For many of us, the first time we hear our voice (on a voicemail recording or a videotape) produces an almost seismic jolt: This surely can't be me, we think. Is this what I really sound like? Chances are what we hear on such a recording is precisely what everyone else who listens to us hears. I continue to be baffled by how many of us do not like the way we sound. We will do anything possible to make sure we do not have to listen to a recording of our voice. This very visceral feeling is caused by a palpable disconnect between how our voice sounds to us, as we speak, and the way it sounds to those who listen to us. Many of us, quite simply, have never heard ourselves.

So, here is where I ask you to begin: Get to know your voice. Record yourself. Listen to your recordings often. Listen to it without judgment. Get used to your voice as it likely sounds to others. Listen to it over and over until you start to accept that this truly is your voice. Through repeated listening, you will quickly reach the point when the sound of your voice no longer feels like an out-of-body visitation from the devil in *The Exorcist*.

This simple act of listening and acceptance can be a truly liberating start. Once we are able to hear our voice as it sounds today—its basic tone, timbre, resonance, and pitch—then we can begin to play with the dimensions of our voice. We will be able to listen for volume, clarity, pace, variety, and speech fillers. We will have the wondrous opportunity to experiment with the range of this voice. We will experiment not because we seek to invent a new, or false, voice. On the contrary, we will discover those qualities of our voice that we have never put to use. We will become the archaeologist who ventures on an exciting new dig—unearthing the truly dynamic voice we have always had.

Here is the good news: Almost any aspect of our voice can be readily shaped, adapted, developed, and modified. And here's even better news: It is very rare that I meet a presenter who needs professional voice correction (and in the event this is necessary, there are numerous experts who can do just that). I intentionally use the verb "play" to describe this process of voice exploration. I want to make sure that discovering our vocal range becomes a light and joyful experience. The starting point is our awareness of the vocal dimensions—they are the many balls we toss in the air, every time we speak. We usually toss them entirely by automatic reflex, with little conscious focus or intent.

In this chapter, we will take a peek at a few of these core vocal dimensions. I have a hunch that as you begin to play with these dimensions, you will also discover new joy in the act of public speaking. And since for many of us "finding our voice" is part of a lifelong quest, we might as well begin with the instrument itself. It is, indeed, a powerful tool.

VOLUME

A few years back, I was applying to be a seminar leader for a consulting firm that coaches executive speakers. The interviewing process consisted of giving several presentations in front of an audience. Now, ever since Joy McLean Bosfield had me breathing from my penis, I have had a voice that resonates. Volume is something I tend to not worry about when I speak. By my second presentation, however, the lead interviewer kindly reminded me that she could not understand what I was saying. This fact was seconded by all the other individuals present in the room.

It happens that quickly. I was under pressure, and I was clearly constricting the flow of breath I needed to support my voice. Moreover, I was startled—I was unaware that I was doing this.

I have coached speaker after speaker who is convinced that he is shouting as he speaks, while the audience is straining to understand the words that fall from his mouth. Of all the disconnects in public speaking, the volume disconnect is the most jarring.

When we speak, we want to project our voice—i.e., send it out to the most faraway members of our audience. Actors spend years in acting school learning to support their voices from their diaphragms. That's what Joy taught me when she was coaching me to breathe down to my groin. The deeper into our bodies we inhale, the more strongly we support our voices, and the more they will resonate. If you have never paid attention to your diaphragm, place your hands over the lower part of your stomach. When you inhale, press that lower part of your stomach visibly forward. When you exhale, push it in as far as you can. You will soon find that the motion resembles the motion of a pump—expanding with an inhale, contracting with an exhale. As you feel this expansion and contraction, know that you have located your diaphragm. If you have a hard time finding your diaphragm, speak with a friend, a colleague, or an acquaintance who sings or has been trained as a singer. Anyone who has ever taken a singing lesson will locate it for you in a flash!

Voices that don't carry well, or voices that produce a consistently high pitch, are usually voices that are not supported from this lower part of the body. If you have been told that you need to speak louder, chances are you have a chest voice. Your inhale tends to stop in the chest area and doesn't reach all the way down to the diaphragm, and you thus miss the vocal power that comes with full diaphragmatic support. In addition, many of us tend to strain in our throat area. If this is a part of your body that tightens under pressure, your voice will be further constrained and not project with maximum volume and resonance.

How do we move our vocal support down to the groin? Well, we are currently blessed with the ever-growing popularity of yoga in this country. Many fitness centers now offer free yoga classes to their members. Yoga is the simplest and most powerful way I know of initiating the practice of deep breathing. Regardless of how deeply you breathe at present, the practice of yoga will help send breath into parts of your body that have for years held only stress and strain. It will gently pry open the channels that support the upward stream of breath throughout your body. Yoga will single-handedly help you to produce a more rounded, full-bodied voice. More importantly, it will help your voice to settle and mature without strain.

Overprojection is a rare occurrence, but once in awhile I actually stumble upon a speaker who shouts at the audience when he speaks. It is frequently a matter of enthusiasm—which is a marvelous quality—pushed over the brink, and suddenly every sentence starts to sound like a decibel assault. Instead of motivating the audience with his enthusiasm, the speaker forces the audience to recoil. The dilemma of the shouter is identical to that of the whisperer—the speaker simply does not hear himself and is unaware of the vocal impact he has on his listeners.

The solution? Practice in front of friends who will help you adjust your volume level. Practice in front of strangers who have no reason not to tell you the truth. Lower your voice for impact. Raise it for emphasis. Lift it a notch or two to draw the audience's attention—at the beginning of a speech, or in response to an external interference. Practice speaking with a lot of distractions around you—this will challenge you to judiciously adjust your volume level and accommodate the distractions. I spent several years facilitating seminars in a hotel in midtown Manhattan. Each seminar unfurled against the soundtrack of the New York City streets—the honking of cars, the whistling of the bellhops, the verbal altercation of pedestrians on the sidewalk. As annoying as these sounds were to seminar participants seeking to deliver the perfect presentation, they actually helped all speakers to modulate their volume. It required constant volume adjustments as it got loud outside. Every speaker was forced to stay conscious of both his volume level and the volume level in the room.

So, much like my clients in this Manhattan hotel, I invite you to toy with your volume levels. Find out first what a comfortable volume level feels like to you. Play with it in different venues. Adjust to the size of the room, the size of your audience, the acoustics of the space, and the level of noise around you and in your audience. Ask your audience members to tell you if they can comfortably hear you. In spite of what many speakers think—the audience is your friend. They want to hear what you have to say, and they will let you know.

CLARITY

Many of us are afflicted with the lazy-mouth disease: Mouths that don't open wide enough to fully articulate the sounds that are imbedded in the words we speak. This can be endearing in a casual social context—hanging out with friends in a café, having a drink in our favorite pub after work. The moment we speak in public, this laissez-faire attitude toward the sound of language forces our audience to work harder than it should. As we surrender our burden of clear communication, we place a larger burden on the shoulders of our audience. Our listeners have to work to fill in the gaps created by the words we don't fully enunciate.

It happens most often at the beginnings and endings of words. We slide into a word and start articulating it halfway through. We leave a word without acknowledging the closing letters. We also do it at the beginning of sentences—we don't start fully articulating until we stumble into the second or third word, and we trail off before a sentence is over. An audience is invariably trying to make sense of what we say. If we consistently forget to enunciate parts of words or entire parts of a sentence, we force the audience to play the role of sleuth. And yes, *we* are the criminals who are aggressively killing the language!

Audience sleuthing is exacerbated by the regional dialects we speak, and the colloquial uses of language that accompany such dialects. Dialects are a rich and delightful part of our language, and I encourage speakers to fully embrace their dialects rather than try to correct or hide them. As an audience member, I enjoy this reminder of the many varied textures of American English. A speaker with a regional dialect that differs from the predominant dialect of her audience, however, needs to pay vigilant attention to the clear articulation of every word. While audiences will often remind her that they find the dialect "charming," truth is they are working a tad harder to understand this "funny accent."

As a non-native speaker for whom English is a second language, I get a special joy out of working with other immigrants who are also presenting in a foreign language. In a global economy, where English has become the world's predominant business language, I encounter more and more business leaders who regularly have to present in a non-native tongue. I am always struck by the deep insecurity many foreigners feel about presenting in English. This insecurity is a double-whammy: non-native speakers have to put more effort into constructing sentences and thoughts in a foreign language, especially if their thinking occurs in their native language. This effort is frequently compounded by a deep-seated fear that their English is not "good enough" and that people will not understand it.

A recent client, Harry Wang, embodied these fears in a rather typical way. He had come to New York from Shanghai, where he worked as the sales manager for Anheuser-Busch in China. He reminded our group of the many different dialects that exist in his country, and told us that, back home, he presented in Mandarin. Every presentation in English began with an apology for his poor command of the English language. This of course was not the case. Harry did, however, have a notable accent that demanded a strong listening effort from his American audience. It was also clear that it was difficult for Harry's tongue to create some of the English sounds, and the construction of certain words presented a very concrete physiological challenge for him. Harry does not need any professional diction correction. But he, like many non-native speakers, needs to assist his audience by keeping his volume raised, by focusing on the clear and complete articulation of all words in a sentence, and by maintaining a pace that is a tad slower than his Mandarin speaking pace.

We reap delicious dividends the moment we start to pay attention to our diction. So often we speak "on automatic" and don't even begin to connect with the words we speak. It is as if the words we utter were the leftovers from a fast-food meal, waiting to be tossed out. Our conscious attention to language and diction challenges us to stay alert. Suddenly, we have the opportunity to actually relish the words we speak. We are able to find nuance and meaning in what we say. Words attain a richness we did not know they had. Almost in spite of ourselves, a little speech soon becomes a four-star dining event, with subtlety and spice and many ravishing flourishes.

PACE

Something happens to many of us the moment we stand up and speak: we start to talk really fast. We don't plan to talk as rapidly as we do—it just happens. It's the devious way in which we try to camouflage our nervousness and insecurity. "If I just talk fast enough maybe they won't notice." The hidden assumption behind a quickened pace is that since everyone is staring at me and hanging on every word I say, I better talk lots and lots and don't ever stop. A rapid-fire delivery, much like sloppy diction, demands an inordinate effort on behalf of the listener to comprehend the speaker's intent. Combine fast pace with sloppy diction, and we have an audience that is working overtime to simply keep up.

Pauses are a powerful and essential part of any presentation. A pause allows the listener to make a personal connection to the words she just heard. A pause invites the listener to relax into a presentation. A pause makes it possible for the speaker to sense the response of an audience to a presentation. Pauses are those beautiful moments when meaning happens and common ground emerges. Because many of us are afraid of pauses and silence, we tend to clutter them with speech-fillers. The "ehms" and "OKs" and "you knows," the coughs, giggles, heavy breaths, and the smacking of our lips. All the sounds we sneak into our speech to banish the silence. What happens, of course, is that the audience invariably begins to listen to the speech-fillers, which have no meaning. The audience notes the distraction instead of the content, and the meaning is diminished until it entirely slips away.

Some speakers dread pauses and silences because they fear that their energy will erode. They equate a fast pace with generating lots of energy. And for many of us this is, in fact, borne out by experience. We find it difficult to maintain energy when we slow down. Seasoned speakers, however, have learned to retain their energy in a moment of silence. They use a pause to both hold the energy of the audience and receive energy from it. Energy is harnessed, and when it is time to continue these speakers are able to sustain the momentum they had before the pause. When they drop or lift their level of energy it is a matter of choice, not because energy has dissipated. And if they choose to deliver at a slower pace they know that they can do so with lots of energy as well.

There certainly are those speakers whose pace is consistently too slow. I encounter this most often in schoolteachers—especially elementary schoolteachers—who suddenly have to present to adults. They have not made either the mental shift or the pace adjustment necessary to talk to a grown-up audience. Everything is delivered at a slow and highly deliberate pace, as if their audience did not have the mental or verbal capacity to comprehend a complete sentence or thought. An overly deliberate pace will invariably be perceived as condescending. The audience really has no choice but to resist the speaker and eventually revolt.

Our goal as we speak is to find variety in our pace. A dynamic presenter does not drone on but modulates her pace. She relishes pauses. She maintains energy regardless of pace. She knows to accelerate her pace when she needs to motivate her audience. Most importantly, she varies her pace in an intuitive manner. She takes her cue from her audience members and their signals of involvement and attentiveness. Her pace is a fluid and ever-changing part of her presentation. This almost-musical sense of pace helps keep the presentation fresh and alive, for her and for everyone in her audience.

EMPHASIS

A choice in emphasis is one of the ways in which a speaker helps an audience make sense of a speech. We can pause before a key word we wish to highlight. We can raise our volume when we pronounce this word. We can stretch the word, slow down the word, elongate the word, linger on key sounds embedded in the word. We can have devilish fun with the words that we speak and emphasize.

In daily speech, our delivery tends to fluctuate between occasional states of excitement and our regular, more-detached way of speaking. In a state of excitement, every word suddenly seems terribly significant and receives emphasis. The result: all emphasis tends to cancel itself out, and the audience receives a generalized rush of excitement. Our habitual everyday delivery frequently lacks any kind of emphasis at all, and is often monotone and flat. For some speakers who use emphasis, inflection consistently occurs at the wrong place in the sentence. Have you ever listened to a speaker who likes to raise his voice at the end of every sentence? The upward lilt makes each sentence sound like a question, even when the speaker is making a declarative statement. Delivered once, it causes the audience to stumble, and becomes a confusing vocal cue. Delivered repeatedly, it becomes an annoying speech pattern that will draw undue attention.

An attention to meaningful emphasis also prevents a speaker from falling into a repetitive language rhythm. An unwavering rhythm sends a strong subliminal message to the audience: "Go take a nap." Repetitive rhythms are often referred to as drones; they are marked by a steady, even spacing between all words. Repetitive rhythms also show up when we start emphasizing words in predictable intervals; suddenly, every fifth word is the word we emphasize, regardless of meaning. My Canadian colleagues and I joke about the penchant of many English-speaking Canadians for sneaking the word "eh" into their sentences. This usually occurs at the end of each sentence. It quickly becomes a rather predictable emphasis pattern. The audience begins to anticipate the "eh rhythm." And yes, it likely will also start to tune out.

I'm often asked whether a speaker should select, in advance, the key words he wishes to emphasize. If emphasis is something that does not come naturally to a speaker, practice and planning may be a great way to ease his mind. It allows for a bit of guaranteed vocal variety. But I suggest we consider it only as a starting point, not as a fixed or rigid goal for the delivery. Meticulously prepared points of emphasis leave the audience out of the equation. Each audience will respond differently to the same presentation. The audience, and its response, will always demand certain shifts in emphasis. And this intuitive sense of what needs to be emphasized with a particular audience is one of the sweet and subtle joys of public speaking.

SELF-AWARE, NOT SELF-CONSCIOUS

The line between self-consciousness and self-awareness is subtle indeed. The purpose of our vocal explorations is certainly not to make us self-conscious. When I am self-conscious, I judge what I do. When I am self-aware, I witness what I do without judgment and know how to adapt and modify.

David Salvatore, for example, is a dynamic speaker who tends to fall on the wrong side of this fine line. He is the highly energetic president of Blair Delmonico, a company that specializes in high-end fashion accessories. The first time we met I noticed nothing unusual about David's voice. A week later, David left a message on my answering machine, and I was startled. The speaker identified himself as David and referred to our prior meeting, but the voice did not sound like it belonged to David. I played the recording back. Four, five times over. With each listening I was more and more convinced that this was a woman's voice. The pitch, the high register, the timbre, the breathiness. Quite frankly, I thought I was the butt of some sort of practical joke.

I decided to call David back to get to the root of this confusing message. When I finally spoke with him, David explained that his voice sometimes jumps into a high register, and that especially over the telephone it frequently gets mistaken for a female voice. "I guess those were the cards I was dealt," David laughed nervously. And then, as if he were making a joke, he dropped his voice into a lower register and proceeded to speak at a slower, more measured pace. The change was dramatic. I immediately heard a different person, and I had a strong hunch that this lower voice was David's authentic voice. He used this voice mockingly, but the fact that he was able to drop his voice told me that he was aware of what his voice did when left unattended. Not only was David self-aware, he could quite effortlessly adapt and speak in a register that did not send a mixed message.

Was his high voice the card he was dealt? No. David needed to stay self-aware and remember what his voice did in moments of stress. Since he was experiencing tremendous pressures in his rapidly growing business, his voice was likely spending a lot of time in his high register and confusing the clients he communicated with all over the world, just as it had confused me. As David and I continued to chat, he talked about the work he had done with a voice coach in Manhattan. The coach apparently had judged his voice quite harshly, and it was immediately evident that David also was a harsh critic of his voice. David had not fully made the switch from self-judgment to self-awareness. Truth was, David knew how to toss the vocal balls. His job, quite simply, was to stay alert under stress and toss them with conscious intent.

As you begin to play with your voice, you will be tempted to judge what you hear. If you do, please remember the beginning of this chapter: Listen to your voice. Hear it as it sounds today. Listen to it, again and again. Embrace it without judgment. And then—start tossing the balls. Toss them with conscious intent. And have fun as you discover how far and wide your vocal tosses will take you!

PRACTICE EXERCISES

Here are three different texts that will guide you in exploring the vocal dimensions we have addressed in this section. Each has a very unique character, tone, and mood. I urge you to investigate all three of these texts rather than just one or two of them. The combination of these texts, and their varied qualities, will help you to stretch your speaking range.

I suggest you first spend some time exploring these texts on your own. After sufficient practice, it will be beneficial to present them to a small audience. In this section, I provide you with suggestions for your solo as well as your small-group practices.

I.

The public outcry over America's failure to generate jobs has focused on the outsourcing of work to China and India. But another dynamic closer to home is weighing on job creation—the slow process of working through a glut of boom-era investment that continues to litter the economy with underused factories. "As long as there is extra capacity available in manufacturing, there is going to be room to move work among companies without adding workers," said Thomas A. Kochan, a Labor and Management expert at the Sloan School of Management of the Massachusetts Institute of Technology. That is true with a vengeance today. Not since the severe recession of the early 1980's has capacity use in manufacturing stayed so low for so long, government data show. Production as a percentage of total capacity fell precipitously in the aftermath of the last recession, with manufacturers on average using less than 73 percent of their capacity.

(from the *New York Times*)

II.

> The wind pulls up his water-spouts
> > His white and foaming breeches;
> He whips the waves; he storms and shouts.
> > The whole sea heaves and pitches!
>
> From the black skies, a furious might
> > Impels the rain's commotion;
> It seems as though the ancient night
> > Had come to drown the ocean.

To the mast a vagrant sea-gull clings
With a hoarse shrilling and crying.
As though in despair she flaps her wings:
An evil prophesying.

(by Heinrich Heine)

III.

Recorded message recently heard in an airport taxi:

"Hello, I am a famous celebrity that you have heard of before—I would like to welcome you to our fair city. As you ride with us, please observe these rules for your safety and comfort.

Rule 1: Please do not speak to the driver while the vehicle is in motion—your voice may distract the driver, creating a potentially unsafe condition or erroneous route to your destination.

Rule 2: Please do not speak to the driver while the vehicle is stopped—your voice may alarm the driver such that he may unexpectedly accelerate, creating the conditions of motion inherent to Rule 1 (see Rule 1).

Rule 3: Please do not look out the windows of the vehicle. Expressing interest in points outside the car may lead the driver to a state of associative curiosity, which may cause him to take his eyes off the road, creating a potentially hazardous condition.

Rule 4: Please do not look at the driver. The driver will feel your eyes upon him and by instinct will want to look back at you, again creating a potentially hazardous condition.

Rule 5: Please do not look in the driver's rearview mirror. For reasons of safety the driver must occasionally glance in this mirror and the chance of your eyes meeting (creating the conditions of Rule 4) are far too great.

Rule 6: Please do not let your feet touch the floor. To better protect our guests from any animal contaminants we ask that you suspend your feet in mid-air until arriving at your final destination.

Rule 7: And finally! Please fasten your seatbelt! We wouldn't want anything to spoil the pleasure of your ride with us! Thank you, and have a great day! This is that celebrity that you have heard of before signing off!"

(by Sam Carter)

Solo Practice

Read each text a few times to get a sense of its tone and perspective. Think of the kind of impact this text intends to have on a listener. To help you capture the different moods of these texts, you may wish to imagine that you are a specific character or personality who has to deliver those words. Imagine what sort of audience you would be addressing with the text.

After this initial exploration, deliver each text a few times over. With each delivery, focus specifically on one of the four vocal dimensions—volume, diction, pace, and emphasis.

Volume

It will help you to conduct your volume practice in a public space, like a park or a sports stadium, at a time when few or no other people are about. To make the volume practice meaningful, deliver the texts to different objects in your vicinity:

- Take a text and say it to a rock that's right in front of you, to a blade of grass just below you, to a tree at a distance, or an electric pole on the opposite end from where you are.
- Speaking to these objects will help you to focus your volume.
- Notice how the blade of grass right beneath you will require a lot less volume than the electric pole in the far distance.
- Get a sense of how little or how much volume you need to talk to each of these objects.
- Notice how your volume changes and adapts to accommodate the varying distances provided by these objects.

Diction

- As you speak these three texts, focus exclusively on fully creating all of the sounds that are in the words of the text.
- Pay attention to fully pronouncing the beginnings and ends of words.
- Pay attention to fully pronouncing the beginnings and ends of each sentence.
- Notice the amount of mouth movement that is required to truly enunciate the language you speak.

Pace

- As you speak each text, note the pace at which you speak.
- Play with both slowing the pace down and speeding it up. Push the slow and fast pace to the extremes. What does it feel like, in your body, to speak very slowly or very rapidly?
- Allow yourself to pause. Languish in the moments when you don't speak. Note what it feels like to not speak.
- Observe any speech fillers that may slip in as you speak.
- Note any physical sensations that you may have in your body as you toy with your speaking pace.

Emphasis

- As you speak the texts, focus on intentionally emphasizing certain words.
- Explore different ways of creating emphasis—by raising your volume, by drawing out the word, by pausing beforehand, by changing your pitch.
- Keep varying the words you emphasize instead of locking into the same ones, every time; note the physical sensations you have as you emphasize core words.
- Note the new meanings and innuendoes that may appear in your texts through your change in emphasis.

Audience Practice

When you feel that you have sufficiently practiced these vocal dimensions on your own, gather an audience and prepare to receive some objective outside feedback. Remember—when it comes to our voice, we don't always hear what others hear, so the feedback from an audience will be invaluable.

Since in many of the practice exercises in this book you will rely on the feedback of an audience, here are some tips to make sure that these exercise sessions will be of value to you:

- Gather three good colleagues or friends around you for each exercise.
- Limit each exercise to a length of ten minutes. Especially when practicing skills with friends or colleagues, it is easy to get side-tracked. A ten-minute time limit gives a manageable focus to each exercise. It will help everyone stay on task.
- Since the exercise is for the benefit of your own speaking development, make sure everyone present understands the purpose of the exercise. Keep the feedback focused on the skill you're developing. Not on how refreshed you look today. Not on how entertaining the story is you're telling (unless that is the particular focus of that practice). Not on how fabulous the sweater you're wearing looks on you. No, we're here to practice specific speaking skills!

Audience Practice Exercises

Select one of the texts that you have practiced. Just as you did when you explored the text on your own, focus on one vocal dimension at a time as you communicate the text to your audience.

Make sure your audience knows what skill you are working on. If, for example, you start with exploring volume, make sure your audience is placed far enough away from you so that you really must project your voice:

- As you speak, focus solely on making sure that your audience can comfortably hear you.
- When you have delivered one entire text, pause for a quick self-observation: How did you do with this skill practice? What went well? What could be improved?
- Elicit some feedback from your audience. Could they comfortably hear you? Was there enough variety in your volume levels? What would help them hear you better?
- Repeat the exercise once or twice more. If your audience gave you specific suggestions for improving your projection, work to integrate their feedback. If they were satisfied with your first delivery, continue to explore the boundaries of your higher and lower volume levels. How softly can you speak and still be comfortably heard? At what point does your projection start to sound unpleasantly loud?
- Repeat the feedback process after each round. Always offer your own feedback first, then listen to the feedback from your audience. And end the ten-minute practice session with an assessment of your strengths in the skill you practiced, as well as any insights on how you would like to further develop your mastery of this skill.
- Repeat a similar process for the other three vocal areas—diction, pace, and emphasis.
- Continue to limit each practice round to ten minutes. Always let your audience know what the focus of your practice is. And continue to explore your range within these vocal dimensions: (1) Explore the difference between overpronunciation and overly casual diction. (2) Explore the difference between a rapid pace and a deliberately slow pace. (3) Explore the difference between no emphasis and overemphasis.
- Remember—this is your opportunity to have a workshop practice without the pressures of a "real-life" audience. It is your chance to take each dimension to the extreme. And, by all means, have fun as you practice!

CHAPTER 2

Body Movement

There is an entire species of public speakers that has become the fodder of MAD-TV skits and late-night talk-show jokes. The kind who, after decades of speaking in public, has morphed into a cultural cliché. I'm referring to the coach who rouses his team. The VP of sales who rallies her reps. The sergeant who fires up the troops. The motivational presenter who "works a stage" with gusto. Charging to one side. Racing back to the other. Moving. Moving. Never standing still.

I call them the preacher-speakers. Hyperkinetic, their every movement seems to assault the audience. They prance. Charge. Stalk. Attack. The motion of their muscles looks like it can be barely contained. Veins seem to pop out of their necks as they speak, and their inner organs appear ready to burst through the walls of their skin. When I watch these speakers strut their stuff, I feel like I am witnessing pure animal energy unleashed. The lion let out of the cage.

Roaming. Circling. Never standing still.

You may look at such a speaker and ask yourself: Am I supposed to move that much when I speak in public? When does body movement cross the line and become *too much* movement? When have I suddenly turned myself into a *caricature* of a speaker?

On the other end of the spectrum is what I will call the mouse. Not the mouse that darts away the moment the light switch is flicked on. No. The *psychological* mouse. The mouse-speaker trembles in stillness and looks as if he had swallowed an overdose of tranquilizers. He stands in one spot and does not ever budge.

Although clearly in plain view of his audience, he wishes he could shun the limelight entirely, crawl into a crack in the floor, and vanish. Instead, he stands in stillness, paralyzed, afraid that any movement will draw more attention to himself.

"If I just stand here and don't move, maybe they won't notice me."

Between the velocity of the lion and the stillness of the mouse lives a whole spectrum of movement choices. In this chapter, we will begin to investigate this spectrum, and the movement vocabulary that best serves a public speaker. Please note that I am separating body movement—the motion of the speaker's body within the presentation space—from the use of gestures—the speaker's expressiveness through the use of arm and hand motion. They are, of course, intricately related, but for the purpose of understanding and honing our movement vocabulary, it will serve us to separate them, just for now. In this chapter, we will look at the use of body movement, and in the subsequent chapter, we will examine the use of gestures.

So where, in the realm of lions and mice, do we find guidelines for a speaker's movement vocabulary? When I pose this question in one of my public-speaking seminars, the first response I invariably receive is this: "Body movement should be appropriate."

Let's agree to this right now: For the remainder of this book we will banish the word "appropriate." *Webster's Dictionary* defines appropriate as both "specially suitable" and "belonging peculiarly." I actually like both of these phrases a good deal. I particularly appreciate the implicit tension between the terms "special" and "suitable," and the terms "belonging" and "peculiar." However, when I hear the term "appropriate" bandied about in a business environment, it usually does not imply special or peculiar. It implies smoothing out a personal speaking style to "fit in" at all cost.

I wish to be unequivocally clear on this matter: Speakers that I hold in high regard are flexible and able to adapt their speaking style to the environment in which they speak. This ability to modify a speaking style is, indeed, the mark of a highly experienced presenter. The term "appropriate," however, is the ultimate expression of cultural relativity. It aims to eradicate any traces of idiosyncrasy and individual quirks. More often than not, it is proposed by speakers who are *appropriately* boring and very adept at putting their audiences to sleep—in a most *appropriate* manner.

This book is about becoming an *exceptional* public speaker. Exceptional public speakers almost always transcend what is appropriate. Exceptional speakers do, however, understand the variables of movement and space, and they know how to use them to their advantage. Movement, and the amount of movement we engage in, will always enhance or diminish the power we hold as the center of attention in a public event.

This is what the seasoned professional knows: Stillness is powerful.

Experienced speakers resist the temptation to move. They understand that staying rooted is a true sign of strength. The attention of the audience is directed toward the speaker anyway, so lots and lots of moving about will actually distract the audience. Audience members will suddenly find themselves observing the movement of the speaker in space. They will note and ponder the dynamics of the movement. If the speaker is graceful, the audience may, indeed, admire the quality of a speaker's motion. The moment they do so, however, they are witnessing the *act* of public speaking instead of receiving the message this act seeks to convey. Unless the message is: "Hey, watch me, I'm a powerful, dynamic speaker."

Think of a moment when you have walked through a meadow, and suddenly found yourself gazing upon a tree. You marveled at the powerful trunk of this tree. You felt its strength and solidity. You could almost sense the energy of the earth surging through the bark of its trunk. Trees have magnificent roots that extend deep into the earth, roots that allow them to be sturdy and seemingly unflappable. If a tree moves at all with the wind, the movement tends to occur in its upper branches, which sway, and in the leaves that give way in the face of a gust.

Such is the power of the rooted speaker. Like a tree that has stood in the same place for decades, she draws attention by simply standing. When she moves she tends to do so with her upper body—turning the torso, inviting with her arms, accentuating with her hands. Her stillness, much like the stillness of the tree, actually allows her to draw on the energy of the earth. It is an energy that calms and grounds her. And it allows her to effectively transform her own physical impulses into expressive and focused upper-body motion.

So, if stillness is so powerful, why does a speaker ever choose to move? Why not stay rooted for the entire duration of a speech? Two variables will usually compel a presenter to integrate more body movement into a presentation. One is the size of the room or auditorium in which she speaks. The other is the intent of the presentation.

In a small meeting room, with an audience of no more than fifteen or twenty people, everyone's attention naturally gravitates toward the speaker. The speaker needs to do little to help focus the audience. The space itself does all of the work, and any unnecessary movement will distract rather than support this natural focus. It will create the impression that the speaker is "working too hard."

In an auditorium where forty or fifty audience members sit in a single row, spanning from one side of a wide hall to the other, a speaker is wise to leave the center of the stage once in awhile and move to its perimeters. The message of the body movement here is very specific and clear: "I know you can all see me, but I haven't forgotten you. I care about you, every one of you. I just want you to know. So let me visit your side of this cavernous hall for a while."

Motion toward an audience says: I care. I want to connect. I want to make sure you understand. Savvy speakers move toward their audience, or a segment of their audience, to forcefully convey this message. The more intent these speakers are on motivating their audience, the more they tend to keep moving toward their audience. Circling away. Moving toward their audience once again. The key to this movement choice is its intent. The speakers are consistently and intentionally, through the use of their body movement, conveying their strong desire to stimulate and ignite their audience.

There's a third variable that much too often comes into play when we observe a speaker's body movement, and that variable is nerves. We may not be able to eradicate nervousness, but we certainly want to eradicate the movements that show up because of it. I am referring to all of those movements of which most speakers are entirely unaware. The unintentional movements that undermine impact and credibility. The little movements that squander energy. The movements that have no purpose whatsoever.

These movements pose a particular challenge for the naturally kinesthetic person—the sort of individual who in every situation in life has a hard time "sitting still." This, however, is the good news: the kinesthetic person has likely been reminded many times in the past of his tendency to fidget. He knows he tends to move too much. He is conscious of his movement foibles. Consciousness is the first step toward modifying our movement excesses. The person who tends to be motionless in most public situations may be entirely unaware that he is making unnecessary movements in the first place. His challenge is to simply begin to notice what he does.

So, what are some of the most commonly seen "nervous" body movements? Here is a by no means exhaustive list of the unintended footwork we want to first notice, then avoid:

- **The shuffle**: The speaker's feet keep moving forward and back, in steady repetition, as if the floor beneath were a bed of burning coal.
- **The sway**: The speaker keeps rocking from side to side, as if standing aboard a ship in the midst of a gathering storm out at sea.
- **The cha-cha**: The speaker's feet move in a repetitious, box-like fashion around the floor, as if he wished to dance with a missing partner.
- **The lean**: The speaker stands on one foot while the other is bent at the knee, with the toes rubbing against the heel of the solid foot as if to soothe a persistent itch.
- **The lift-off**: The speaker rises up on the toes, at least once in every sentence, as if preparing for the high jump.
- **The cross**: The speaker's legs cross at the ankles, as if a dash to the toilet is imminent and unavoidable.

- **The bop**: The speaker's legs wiggle and hop in place, as if an army of ants were marching down his legs in a slow and steady crawl.
- **The step-away**: The speaker is consistently performing little steps away from the audience, as if the audience were the beast that had just escaped its cage at the zoo.

In the upcoming exercises, we will have the opportunity to practice the key aspects of focused body movement: we will experience the power of rooted speaking. We will look at how we harness our body energy by using intentional movement. At the same time, we will have a chance to observe the little unintentional movements that often creep up as we speak. And finally, we will look at ways of using body movement to help shift and direct the focus of our audience!

PRACTICE EXERCISES

Just as you did in the second half of your vocal exercises, gather an audience of three friends or colleagues for this practice round. It is difficult to explore body movement without being in a spatial relationship to an audience. And since body movement is frequently the sort of movement of which we are entirely unaware, the observations of an audience will be crucial in making us conscious of what the body does, and what our body movements communicate to our audience.

Once again, plan to limit each exercise to a length of ten minutes. And as you did in your previous exercises, make sure your audience knows your personal focus for each of the practice rounds.

Exercise 1: Rooted Power

In this exercise, you will practice staying rooted in one place without unnecessarily moving about. If you like imagery, imagine that the soles of your shoes are glued to the floor on which you stand.

It is potent glue, and it would require superhuman efforts from you to tear yourself away from this spot.

If you are a speaker who likes to stroll and wander, this exercise may at first feel constraining. That, of course, is its point. A focus on "staying glued" forces us to become conscious of all the little movements that our feet long to execute across the floor. Especially when we're nervous, this is where the "nervous dance" occurs. By practicing *rooted* power, you will start to experience the subtle inner shifts that happen as you harness your *movement* power. And you will learn not to squander this power in unintentional ways.

- Pick a topic that you can comfortably talk about for three minutes. The content is irrelevant. To help you practice rooted power it is useful to talk about something you know well—this allows your focus to go toward staying rooted rather than having to think about what to say next.
- As you speak, focus solely on staying rooted in the place where you began your speech. You may find that you have strong impulses to leave the spot. Resist these impulses, and notice what happens to your energy as you choose not to move.
- When your three minutes are over, pause for a quick self-observation: How did you do with this skill practice? What went well? What could be improved?
- Elicit feedback from your audience. Were they able to see you staying rooted? Did they see you engage in any other movements of which you may have been unaware?
- Repeat the exercise once or twice more, this time speaking for only two minutes at a time. Remember—the focus of this exercise is not to entertain your friends with your stories but to get a physical sensation of what it feels like not to move. Your goal is to create a new body memory for yourself—the memory of what it feels like to stay rooted, and how this rootedness affects the energy in your body.
- Repeat the feedback process after each round. Always offer your own feedback first, then listen to the feedback from your

audience. And end the ten-minute practice session with an assessment of your strengths in the skill you practiced, as well as any insights on how you would like to further develop your mastery of this skill.

- I urge you to stick to the same content in each of the three practice rounds. This will help you, and your audience, to focus on the skill you are practicing: staying rooted as you speak.

Exercise 2: Choosing Intentional Movement

For this exercise, feel free to move about if the spirit moves you. As you move, make sure you move because you wish to better engage one of your audience members or your entire audience. Try to avoid those little unintentional movements we talked about earlier—the cha-cha, the lean, the sway, the step-away, to mention just a few. They tend to have a will of their own and like to sneak in unannounced.

This will be the focus for your audience during this practice: Ask your friends to watch for the amount of body movement you generate. Is it too much? Too little? Does it help them focus, or do they find it distracting? Does it look like intentional movement, or do they notice any of the unintentional movements we wish to avoid?

- Once again, pick a topic you can comfortably talk about for three minutes. To help you practice your body movement, it is useful to talk about something you know well—this way your concentration is more likely to go toward your body movements and not the topic of your mini-presentation.
- As you speak, focus solely on moving with intent: Moving toward audience members to engage them. Moving away to open up to the entire group. Explore what it feels like to alternate between moments of rooted stillness and moments of intentional movement. And be mindful of any unintentional movements that may sneak in. Becoming aware of such movements will allow you to adapt and modify your movement choices.

- When your three minutes are over, pause for a quick self-observation: How did you do with this skill practice? What went well? What could be improved?
- Elicit feedback from your audience members. What were their perceptions of your movement choices? Did your movements look like purposeful movement to your audience? Did they notice any distracting, unintentional movements?
- Repeat the exercise once or twice more, this time speaking for only two minutes at a time. Remember—the focus of this exercise is your exploration of intentional movement, and your ability to distinguish between nervous and purposeful movement choices. And if you have received feedback about any unintentional movements, your goal is to banish those movements from your movement vocabulary.
- Repeat the feedback process after each round. Always offer your own feedback first, then listen to the feedback from your audience. And end the ten-minute practice session with an assessment of your strengths in the skill you practiced, as well as any insights on how you would like to further develop your mastery of this skill.

Exercise 3: Moving for Focus

Experienced presenters know to use movement as a simple and elegant way of drawing the audience's attention. A body movement may be initiated to signal an important point in a story. It may be used to redirect an inattentive audience member. It can be deployed to divert the audience from an external distraction. Since movement always draws attention, we will take a peek at how it can be used as a subtle strategic tool to command attention.

You certainly will use this tool spontaneously in many public-speaking situations. For the purpose of this exercise, however, it may be helpful to anticipate using it three times during your three-minute presentation. Select a topic you have addressed in a prior presentation, and select three moments when you will make a move to strongly focus the audience on you or a point in the story. You will know that you are successful when you see your audience "perk up" as you make your move. The move will be especially compelling if the audience doesn't know that this was your reason for moving. Typical moves for focus involve moving toward center stage, moving toward a part of the stage area that you have not visited before, or moving closer to the audience than you have at any previous point in your presentation.

- As you speak, remain rooted until you reach those moments when you choose to "move for focus." As you move, observe the audience's reactions to your move. Notice any inner reactions you may have as you intentionally shift focus. Do you enjoy drawing focus? What happens within you as your audience watches you move? And continue to be mindful of the little nervous movements that might take hold.

- When your three minutes are over, pause for a quick self-observation: How did you do with this skill practice? What went well? What could be improved?

- Elicit feedback from your audience members. What were their perceptions of your movement choices? Did your movement help draw their attention? Did they understand the purpose of your movement? Were they distracted by any of your movements?

- Repeat the exercise once or twice more, this time speaking for only two minutes at a time. Remember—you are exploring the power of movement to draw focus. Your movements may be bold or very small indeed. As you choose your focusing movements, continue to explore the different ways in which you can move through your presentation area.

- Repeat the feedback process after each round. Always offer your own feedback first, then listen to the feedback from your audience. Again, end the ten-minute practice session with an assessment of your strengths in the skill you practiced, as well as any insights on how you would like to further develop your mastery of this skill.

CHAPTER 3

Gestures

I have a memory of sitting with my mom and dad over dinner in a Spa Hotel in the Sauerland region of Germany. It was a traditional, restrained German dining room, where the women who waited on the tables dashed about in quiet servitude and the other guests ate their dinners while engaged in hushed conversation. At one point during our table chat I got excited about a turn in the conversation. I noticed how my voice suddenly lifted a notch above the hum in the room, and my arms began to gesture with enthusiasm in the air above my plate of steamed vegetables.

"Don't get so excited," my mother said to me with a look of worry and consternation.

I was not a child when this was said to me. I was an adult in his early forties.

The moment was unexpectedly poignant for me because I realized, right then, that I had received many comparable messages about how expressive I should be. I had received them for years. Messages about the way I use my voice, and messages about the way I gesture in public.

It occurred to me as well that every client I coach has received similar signals about how expressive he or she is allowed to be. The beauty of my mother's statement to me was that it was so clear and explicit. But as we grew up, all of us received countless implicit messages about the manner in which we should communicate with the world. We observed to what extent others around us were expressive. We also noted how non-expressive they were. We heard the comments Mom made about Aunt Dora who got too wild at parties, flailing and gesticulating out of control. We heard Dad mock Uncle Joe who was just a bit too flashy and flamboyant with his gestures, "for a man." And we internalized many of these implicit messages and molded our own style accordingly. For the majority of us, this meant only one thing: We made sure we didn't stick out from the crowd. We stopped expressing.

This is a comment I have heard more than once from a client: "You know, where I come from we all talk real loud, and we all speak with our hands and arms." More often than not, such a comment is uttered by an individual who stems from a culture that is commonly considered expressive. A Mediterranean culture, for example, or a Latino culture. Invariably, when it is his turn to speak, he is neither very loud, nor does he use his hands and arms to gesture. His posture, in fact, is invariably rather stiff, and his hands hide uncomfortably behind his back or clasp in front of his chest in variations on the prayer position.

I used to wonder: So what happened to the expressive side of this man? Why is he not using his arms to gesture, if that's what he saw every day back home?

My initial answer invariably was, "Well, it must be a case of the nerves." (We'll talk more about nerves and nervousness later). But then it dawned on me that, more likely, a whole other dynamic was coming into play. Along with the messages we receive at home, we receive a second set of implicit signals the moment we join the workforce. Signals about what it means to look and act like a professional. Usually we interpret these signals somewhat like this: OK, if I want to succeed here I better not do anything to draw undue attention to myself. If I have to speak at a meeting I better not get too flashy. I'll keep it cool. No out-of-control behavior. Certainly no wild gestures.

This concern about being viewed as a professional speaker is especially prominent in many female presenters I coach. Individuals who in casual conversation are animated, gesture with ease, and positively bubble with physical expression, suddenly become stiff and closed before an audience. My colleague Lynne Hurdle-Price, a gifted teacher and conflict-resolution specialist, explained it to me as follows: "You know what the stereotype about women is, don't you? That we're way too emotional about everything! So when it comes time to speak, we reign it in. We don't even know that we're doing it, but we do it. We don't want to be seen as the overly emotional ones. So we overcompensate and go full steam the other way. We step into the professional box."

Every one of us—female and male—is guided by such deeply embedded mental imprints. Behind these imprints lurks the unspoken fear that, when we present in public, we may get carried away and "go too far." So we do whatever we can to control this fear. Going too far can show up in the choice of words that we utter. Some speakers control this by always sticking to a prepared script. It can show up in the way in which we use body movement. Some speakers control this by standing still—which, as you remember from the previous chapter, can be powerful if we use stillness as an intentional choice, not out of fear. And the fear of overgesturing—well, we tend to control that by not gesturing at all.

True, we won't offend anyone that way.

It's also unlikely that we'll engage or inspire anyone.

I still encounter presenters who have been told by a speaking coach not to gesture at all. This makes me livid. An audience is entitled to an expressive presenter, and this includes the speaker's use of gestures. Whenever I ask a group of clients to help me define to what extent a speaker should gesture, the answer I receive 99 percent of the time is this: "Gestures should look natural."

I agree.

Now here is where this simple, little adjective becomes a tad complicated. The fortunate presenters are, indeed, "natural" gesturers who use their gestures without much deliberate consideration. Their hands just tend to want to move and help express the intent of their presentation. Their gestures are not timid. Their gestures have an intuitive variety and ease to them. They are constant without drawing too much attention to themselves.

If you are such a speaker, count your blessings. It is your job, quite simply, not to lose this ease of expression once you speak in front of a group. Trust your gestures. Don't tinker with them. Don't stop the flow just because you have an audience.

Some speakers are naturally inexpressive. Left to their own devices, they will simply not gesture at all. Should they continue to speak without gesturing, since this is their natural way of expressing? I think not. Chances are there is a whole other range of expression through and with the use of gestures that these speakers have not experienced. Their body has no kinesthetic memory of attempting certain hand and arm motions. Gesturing is like a foreign language that has not been mastered. Can this foreign language be learned? Can it be learned with a degree of fluency? Sure. If you are such a speaker, I urge you to start experimenting with a wider movement range. Be willing to transcend what is naturally comfortable for you.

Other speakers gesture with movements that are small and floppy. Their natural gestures look as though their motion were cut off at the elbows. Their hand motions don't extend into the upper body; they resemble those of a bird with broken wings, ready to take off and trying to do so with muscles that simply won't comply. Small gestures are, indeed, natural for such speakers. These gestures will, however, do little to help engage an audience. They will, at best, be perceived as awkward. More likely, they will cause the audience to rapidly dismiss the speaker as incompetent and tune him out.

Even if we are presenters who gesture freely, we want to make sure that the gestures we use help to draw in our audience. I recently coached a very engaging young man who was naturally expressive and very energetic. Alan frequently used gestures where one fist would punch or slap the palm of his other hand. These gestures came across as forceful, aggressive, almost like attacks. When we paused to reflect on this choice of gesture, Alan commented that he was an avid baseball player and played on a team every morning before coming to work. He recognized that these were the kind of gestures that came from the sport he so enjoyed. His audience members in this seminar, however, were all females and not the buddies on his baseball team. They perceived his gestures as a bit too aggressive. Were these gestures natural for Alan? Sure. However, they had an alienating impact on this particular audience. After this moment of awareness, Alan was readily able to adapt his gestural inclinations.

When I speak, for example, I have a tendency to gesture with both hands at the same time. Moreover, both of my hands always long to perform the very same gesture. I call this gesturing "in stereo." Many speakers like to use stereo gestures to emphatically support a statement. A little bit of gesturing in stereo, however, goes a long way. Consistent stereo-gesturing may be perceived as aggressive or overly dramatic. My little "aha" moment occurred when a coach pointed out this pattern to me, and reminded me that it was quite OK to gesture with only one hand, once in awhile, and let the other rest. It was not something that I instinctually did. It required a little bit of conscious effort. This small observation, however, has greatly enhanced the range and variety of my hand gestures.

Especially in business environments, it is at times essential for a leader to project unwavering confidence and authority. Business leaders, executives, politicians, and media personalities have often been encouraged by their coaches to use sharp, staccato gestures when they speak. Such gestures tend to have a definitive quality. They resemble a quick, deliberate, omnipotent slash through the air. They tend to say, "Look, I'm in charge. Don't even think of questioning what I'm saying." Such gestures will, indeed, do the trick. They are the equivalent of a quick power-makeover. A word of caution, however: these gestures are rarely authentic and frequently clichéd. They are usually not the sort of gestures any of us use in everyday life. Unless the speaker is also able to connect with an inner sense of confidence and power, such gestures will invariably create the impression that the speaker is mechanical and, worse yet, utterly inauthentic.

Is it possible to gesture too much? Sure. There can be situations when too much gesturing will be in conflict with the tone of a meeting. If I am announcing unwelcome business news at a stockholders' meeting or if I am delivering a eulogy at a best friend's funeral, an overly animated body language may be misconstrued as entirely out of sync with the mood of the occasion. If I am presenting in a less-expressive culture, an overly gestural style may actually be viewed as showing disrespect toward the audience. In my coaching experience, however, I rarely come across the presenter who needs to "tone down" her or his gestures. Most of us have an overdeveloped internal "gesture meter," and it usually has done far too good of a job of negating our gesture vocabulary.

For many presenters, it is more of a challenge to figure out what to do with their arms and hands when they don't wish to gesture. The easiest, and most obvious, resting position is the one that we tend to resist the most: simply standing and letting our arms dangle at our sides. Why is this one so tough? We're most vulnerable and exposed when we stand like this. We're not using gestures to hide or camouflage. We're not doing anything, and as a speaker it is easy to feel the pressure to be busy at all times.

What about cupping the hands in front of our bodies when we don't wish to gesture? It is a popular resting spot with many presenters. Beware, however, of staying in this position for long. It will tempt you to suddenly rub or grind the palms of your hand, or engage in a multitude of other little nervous hand movements. It is a position you likely never find yourself in when you don't speak in front of a group. For most folks I know it is not a "natural" position but rather one that seems to have been imported purely for the purposes of public speaking. Furthermore, it creates a subtle but clear barrier between you and your audience. It is also best to avoid clasping your hands behind your back. Yes, it allows us to hide any nervous hand motions. But most of us look rather goofy this way. Like the kid who never quite grew up.

And here are a couple of final, gender-specific alerts: Male presenters, especially, like to slide their hands into their pants pockets for a brief rest. It is a safe, comfortable position for many men. It makes us feel casual and relaxed. Well, here is an emphatic veto to ever putting your hands in your pockets while you speak. We hide when we tuck our hands away, and the act of public speaking is inherently about being seen, not hiding. Hands in your pockets may be interpreted as being overly familiar, not respectful, cocky, or a little insecure by an audience. It is also frequently cumbersome to yank the hands back out of the pockets. It makes it virtually impossible to flow with grace from gesturing to non-gesturing. Female presenters who like to wear jewelry—especially arm bracelets—need to be sensitive to any sound distractions this may create. The moment we gesture, jewelry will move, and if we wear multiple pieces of jewelry we have suddenly become a speaker who is backed by a clanking, tinkling jewelry chorus.

This, then, will be our goal as we develop our gestural range:

- We want to use a variety of gestures
- We want to know what our comfortable resting positions are
- We want to use gestures that support our intended message
- We want to use gestures that are inviting
- We want to remember that there is not just one right gesture, or one right way of gesturing

Above all, we want to become intuitive gesturers who do not have to think too hard about our gestures. To reach this state of gestural ease, we may need to be counterintuitive for a while and explore a broader gesture range until that range begins to feel utterly natural and unforced, as if it was how we had always expressed ourselves.

PRACTICE EXERCISES

Just as it has been with every skill we have practiced so far, our sense of how we gesture may be entirely different from how our audience perceives our gestures. So, gather three friends or colleagues about you for some practice sessions to help you explore your gestural range. With each round, make sure your audience clearly understands your goals for that particular practice. And continue to limit a practice round to about ten minutes; this will help make each round manageable and assure that your audience maintains its focus.

Exercise 1: Claiming Your Resting Position

For many speakers, knowing what to do with their hands when they don't wish to gesture can be as stressful as figuring out what to do with them when they actually *want* to gesture. In this first exercise, gesture freely when the spirit moves you, but in between bursts of gestural activity bring your arms to your side to rest. This is the most natural resting position, and for many speakers the most uncomfortable one as well. We feel naked when we stand with our arms dangling by our sides. We will be tempted to counteract this sense of vulnerability by hunching our shoulders, constricting our chest, or finding a myriad ways of holding our hands clasped in front of our body. As you speak, allow yourself to settle into this natural resting position, and notice what your body wishes to do as you stay in this position for a while.

- Pick a topic you can comfortably talk about for three minutes. You want to direct your attention toward observing the flow between gesturing and holding your resting position, rather than worrying about the topic of your mini-presentation.
- As you speak, gesture freely but then find ways of bringing your arms and hands to your sides. Let them drop freely. Notice how it feels to simply stand in front of your audience without engaging in gestures. Watch for all the little adjustments your body seeks to make as you stand. Continue to alternate between gesturing and settling back into your resting position. Stay mindful of your physical impulses as you simply stand and choose not to gesture.
- When your three minutes are over, pause for a quick self-observation: How did you do with this skill practice? What went well? What could be improved?
- Elicit feedback from your audience members. Ask them to focus on their experience of your resting positions, rather than their

perceptions of your gestures. Did you look relaxed when you didn't gesture? Did they notice any discomfort in you when you "simply stood?" Did any unintentional movements sneak in during your resting moments?

- Repeat the exercise once or twice more, this time speaking for only two minutes at a time. Remember—the focus of this exercise is the exploration of your resting position, and your ability to make this a comfortable place to come back to, again and again. Continue to find relaxed ways of settling into this neutral stance. Sometimes simply revisiting this position, time after time, will help it to feel more natural.
- Repeat the feedback process after each round. Always offer your own feedback first, then listen to the feedback from your audience. And end the ten-minute practice session with an assessment of your strengths in the skill you practiced, as well as any insights on how you would like to further develop your mastery of this skill.

Exercise 2: Exploring Gestural Variety

Now that you are becoming comfortable with resting your arms and hands by your sides, let us explore the movement range of your gestures. Many of us tend to fall into repetitive gestural patterns, so here are some ways in which you can play with your gestures:

- Rounded, circular gestures are often perceived as inviting—they help extend your personal energy to the group.
- Sharp and pointed gestures can work well to emphasize key points—they may also be perceived as assertive and quite possibly aggressive.
- Small gestures can be extended and made more expansive.
- Expansive gestures can be reigned in and contained.
- Abrupt, staccato gestures can be smoothed and rounded out to become more inviting.

- Gestures that are small and timid can be "liberated" by including more of your elbows in the movement.
- Persistent stereo-gesturing can be modified by once in awhile gesturing with only one hand and resting the other.

Especially when we gesture, what feels "natural" to us may not always look very natural or inviting to our audience. So don't be afraid to toy with gestures that may fall outside of what you normally do—you may discover some wonderful ways of self-expressing that very soon will feel completely natural.

- Pick a topic you can comfortably talk about for three minutes. As you speak, gesture freely and stay aware of all the different ways in which you gesture. Explore ways in which you can extend and contain your gestures. Experiment with gestures that will draw your audience into the content of your presentation. Try gestures that will emphasize key points of your topic.
- When your three minutes are over, pause for a quick self-observation: How did you do with this skill practice? What went well? What could be improved?
- Elicit some feedback from your audience members. Ask them to comment on the specific quality of your gestures. Did they find your gestures inviting? Did they see enough variety in your gestures? Did your gestures seem to flow effortlessly? What would help make your gestures look more natural?
- Repeat the exercise once or twice more, this time speaking for only two minutes at a time. Remember—the focus of this exercise is the exploration of your gestural range. Continue to find new ways of using your arm and hand motions to invite your audience and create emphasis. Incorporate any specific coaching tips you may have received from your audience members.
- Repeat the feedback process after each round. Always offer your own feedback first, then listen to the feedback from your audience.

And end the ten-minute practice session with an assessment of your strengths in the skill you practiced, as well as any insights on how you would like to further develop your mastery of this skill.

Exercise 3: Using Gestures to Tell a Story

Expert storytellers love to use their gestures to illustrate the events in a story. The gestures, quite literally, bring the story "to life." This is the most overt and extravagant way of using gestures. If you are someone who likes to get dramatic when you tell a story, you likely use illustrative gestures without giving it a second thought. If, on the other hand, you are a speaker who shies away from gesturing a lot, this illustrative use of gestures may feel quite grand and over the top.

Either way, this storytelling approach can be wonderfully liberating for any speaker. It is the simplest way I know to leap beyond our small gestural boundaries. You will be surprised by the motions and gestures the story elicits from you. And as you let yourself go, you will discover how much fun it can be to shamelessly use your hand and arm and—yes—whole body movements to bring a moment to life.

- Select a brief personal story that has a lot of drama or action in it. A mishap, an accident, a small personal disaster, especially if it involves dealing with physical obstacles or clear visceral sensations—such moments are fertile ground for evocative and expressive storytelling.
- As you tell the story, embellish the details. This is not an exercise in understated delivery. Blow by blow you want to use your gestures, arm motions, and your entire body if necessary, to vividly re-create the events of the story!
- When your story has been told, pause for a quick self-observation: How did you do with this skill practice? What went well? What could be improved?
- Elicit feedback from your audience members. Ask them if your gestures helped bring the story to life. Were your gestures bold

enough? Were there additional parts to the story where gestures would have enhanced their listening experience? How did the gestures help to draw them into your story?

- Repeat the exercise once or twice more. Chances are the first time around was merely your warm-up. So as you tell the same story again, find added ways to use gestures as well as body movement to enhance your presentation. Keep surprising yourself! Use the exercise as an opportunity to shamelessly ham it up! And incorporate any specific coaching tips you may have received from your audience members.

- Repeat the feedback process after each round. Always offer your own feedback first, then listen to the feedback from your audience. And end the ten-minute practice session with an assessment of your strengths in the skill you practiced, as well as any insights on how you would like to further develop your mastery of this skill.

CHAPTER 4

Eye Contact

They say it about Bill Clinton, and they said it about Ronald Reagan. These are men of different personalities, with divergent worldviews, yet both are often mentioned in the same breath by coaches and audiences alike as examples of great communicators. There are multiple reasons for this reputation, I'm sure, but as I watch these two leaders speak I marvel at the astonishing finesse with which they apply two very specific skills: they both know how to pause to great effect, and they know how to hold eye contact. Truly, unflinchingly, hold it and sustain it.

I witnessed this same level of "eye contact power" when I spent seven months in Israel, during the early part of 1998, spearheading a project for the Shimon Peres Center for Peace. The first time I experienced the presence of Mr. Peres was during a quick meet-and-greet in a little vestibule of the Grand Park Hotel in Ramallah. Ushered in by his press secretary, every move by Mr. Peres was carefully orchestrated as his secretary motioned him toward this and that individual in the tiny room. What awed me at once was the clear, fearless, almost haunting gaze with which Mr. Peres approached every person he met. It was quite evident that each encounter was to last no more than twenty, thirty seconds. And the individuals who Mr. Peres was meeting in this little vestibule were not other politicians or celebrities or anyone he was likely ever to meet again. Yet for those few seconds Mr. Peres delivered steady, focused, unwavering eye contact. The sort of eye contact that could melt icebergs and move mountains.

It is, of course, not entirely fair to hold such world leaders up as the benchmark. They command attention, partially, because they possess institutional authority and power. A speaker without the same institutional clout may have to work a bit harder to win comparable respect, interest, and attention. But these leaders show us, so compellingly, why eye contact is such a powerful tool.

A comment I frequently hear from my clients is that leaders such as Clinton and Reagan or Peres are natural communicators. No, fellow power speakers! These skills have been carefully practiced, honed, refined, and assimilated. These three individuals are master communicators because the manner in which they use eye contact is so entirely integrated into the way in which they approach whomever they meet. It is no longer a trick or technique. It is their standard for communicating with anyone and everyone. It has, indeed, become their natural way of communicating.

The funny part about eye contact is this: Speakers who don't make a lot of eye contact don't know that they don't make eye contact. They are not aware that there is this whole other level of communicating with an audience. They haven't experienced the thrill of sustained eye connection.

I want to entice you to join me on this thrill ride. The moment I make eye contact with an audience member, the communication is no longer simply about what I, the speaker, am saying. It's about how it is received, and the exchange of giving and receiving. Eye contact changes every communication. It forces me to get real. It jolts me out of the rut of the canned speech, because the moment I make eye contact—the kind of eye contact where I acknowledge the person whose eyes I meet—I have to let in what that person is sending back. Interest. Enthusiasm. Boredom. Confusion. His or her reaction suddenly informs, in ways I won't always control, the next thing I say and the way in which it is said. It turns every presentation into a dynamic exchange. New. Fresh. Alive.

I witnessed Mr. Peres use eye contact to such effect in the context of the repeated one-on-one encounter. But how do we harness the power of this intimate eye-to-eye connection and transfer it to the experience of speaking in front of an entire group? Can we hold and sustain eye contact in such a way that every member of the audience feels personally spoken to, whether it is an audience of fifteen or fifty or five hundred? And if this is, indeed, such a self-evident and powerful tool, why doesn't the world of public speaking brim with commanding speakers who consistently deliver great eye contact?

Let's take a look at some of the myths and misconceptions about the use of eye contact. There isn't a week in my life as a coach that I don't hear some or all of these misconceptions. They are part of the inner dialogue many speakers engage in—the sort of dialogue that prevents them from fully applying the tools available to them. I propose we air some of the myths, dust them off a little, and do a bit of mental housecleaning before we focus on how we want to practice and integrate eye contact.

Myth #1: Some people don't like to receive eye contact. It frightens them and they feel put on the spot.
Guess what—this statement is likely a lot more about your fear as a speaker than the fear of the audience member. An audience member wants to be drawn in. Even if his body language says, "I don't want to sit in this meeting or listen to the presentation." No one likes to be bored. Everyone, ultimately, longs to be engaged. It is my job as a speaker to engage him, and offering eye contact is one of the most powerful ways of accomplishing just that.

Yes, if my intention is to intimidate or antagonize the audience member, he'll look away. But we're not talking about staring someone down, or giving him the evil eye. The intent behind the eye contact needs to be clear and consistent: I invite you to join me. I want to connect with you. I want you to understand why our topic is important. I know what I'm saying will have a tangible impact on your life.

Myth #2: If you're nervous at the beginning of a presentation, don't look at the audience but look slightly above their heads!
Rubbish—you'll just stay nervous this way. The blank wall in the back of the room is not your friend. It will not relax you or

take the nervousness away. It will keep you talking into a void. It will, in fact, accelerate the anxiety in your head and tighten the knot in your stomach, because, moment by moment, you will be creating a speech that is truly not arriving anywhere. The only way to start easing nervousness is to turn a monologue into a conversation. Right away. Find a friendly face in the crowd. Lock eyes with the individual. Receive her eye contact. The anxiety will start to fade. Guaranteed.

Myth #3: The best way to make eye contact with an audience is to consistently scan the room.
This is what coaches taught speakers fifteen or twenty years ago. I call it the "retro"—and mind you, not retro-chic—school of eye contact management. The practice of scanning sharply delineates the generation gap in the public speaking cycle of life. Now, please don't misunderstand me—a little bit of scanning is, indeed, a desirable thing. By "scanning," I refer to the practice of letting the eyes roam wide across the audience so every audience member feels addressed by the speaker. This, however, is the fear: The eyes will be tempted to race around the room as if the speaker were on speed. They will want to "run away" with the speech. Quite literally so.

This fear is based on watching speaker after speaker who has been coached the scanning way. Their eyes soon begin to resemble a pair of airplanes high above a busy airport, circling and circling, waiting in vain for traffic control to give them permission to land. Imagine being the pilot who has to navigate such a flight—a flight that has taken off and then never, ever lands! Scan a bit if you must. But let your eyes settle on one person. Stay for a sentence or a thought. Direct your eye contact to another audience member. Connect. Move on. Connect with someone else. Move on.

This sounds simple, doesn't it? Well—the alternative approach I just outlined invariably leads us to another myth.

Myth #4: If I don't scan, I won't be able to give everyone the impression that I'm including them.
Sure you will. By looking at one person with intent, that individual will know that you are making direct eye contact with him.

The unexpected side benefit is that the folks sitting in the vicinity of this individual will feel like you are talking directly to them as well. Why is this so? You are, after all, not looking directly at them!

Sustained eye contact with one individual strongly and compellingly channels all of our energy to that part of the room. Scanning, on the other hand, consistently scatters our energy throughout. We think we're addressing everyone as we scan. The impact, usually, is entirely the opposite: No one feels as if they are truly spoken to.

Folks sitting around the person receiving sustained eye contact will experience you much more strongly through that act of eye contact than if your eyes were to pass over them for a moment and move on. They will feel like they are receiving your personal eye contact as well, while what they are actually experiencing is the laser focus of your energy, which is clear, direct, and undiluted. Sustained personal eye contact is, indeed, the most economical way of addressing and engaging an entire cluster in your audience.

Myth #5: I can't possibly hold eye contact all the time. I have to look away when I don't know what to say.
Let me rephrase this myth just a bit. For many of us, it feels like a natural instinct to look away when we don't know what to say. This is often the moment when we feel most vulnerable—we're at a sudden loss for words. We feel flustered and panicked. We feel that whoever we look at can see right through us.

It is, in a way, our most powerful moment as a speaker. It so brilliantly illustrates the two tracks we always walk when we speak: We're connecting with an audience member, and we are at the same time creating the next word, the next sentence, the next line of thought. Consistently walking both tracks is a challenge for any speaker whose presentation is not "canned." The moment we look away, however—to the floor, the ceiling, wherever our eyes choose to go—we give away part of our power. I invite you to hold on to your power. Stay connected to a member of your audience. Fearlessly, shamelessly, even when the next sentence hasn't materialized yet.

Myth #6: In some cultures, eye contact is considered rude and offensive. I don't want to offend anyone with my eye contact.

Yes—there are cultures where it is considered impolite to stare at folks directly. Should you deliver a speech in Korea, for example, you may wish to temper the frequency and intensity of your eye contact. But honestly, how often are you in Seoul, delivering a presentation in front of an exclusively Korean audience?

I don't mean to be glib with this observation. As someone who grew up in a European culture, has traveled and worked in many parts of the world, and now resides in the United States, I greatly appreciate the need to be sensitive to the different cultural signals and norms that I encounter. But make no mistake about it: in the overwhelming amount of business scenarios, especially in this intensely globalized world, the communication standard is uniform. Offering strong eye contact signals "I care about you, my audience member." Violating this implicit norm will, in the end, be interpreted as rude behavior—not the other way around.

Myth #7: It is impossible to give eye contact in a darkened room, when I cannot see my audience.

True—there are rooms where you, the speaker, are on stage, and the lights in the auditorium are dim. I know presenters who actually long for this kind of room arrangement. It allows them to deliver a speech as planned, without the distraction of having to respond to the body language of the audience.

But who says the lights in the auditorium or room must stay completely dark? Who decided that this is the way you will deliver your presentation? I have never presented in a room where a light adjustment was impossible. It is part of my responsibility as a presenter to create the best possible conditions for impacting my audience. A dark room deprives me of a major opportunity to connect. It, in fact, sends a strong indirect message to my audience: Take a nap, because I'm not very interested in seeing you anyway. So, please adjust the physical circumstances of your presentation. Remove the darkness barrier. Bring in some candles. Pull aside the shades. Find the light switch. Turn on the lights!

PRACTICE EXERCISES

You will definitely need a little bit of outside assistance to practice eye contact. It is difficult to practice eye contact without someone to look at. Making eye contact with yourself in the mirror—while certainly an enlightening self-development exercise—won't quite do the trick. Gather three good friends or colleagues around you for each exercise and continue to limit each exercise to a length of ten minutes. Make sure that everyone present understands the purpose of the exercise, and keep the feedback focused on the skills you're developing.

Exercise 1: Holding Eye Contact for a Complete Sentence or Thought

In this exercise you will practice holding and sustaining eye contact with an audience member. Especially when we're nervous, our eyes, too, want to engage in a nervous dance. They want to flicker, dart, and flit all over the room. They will do anything not to settle down. This exercise will give you the experience of creating steady, focused eye contact that truly supports the clear communication of your content.

- Pick a topic that you can comfortably talk about for three minutes. The content is irrelevant. To help you practice sustained eye contact, it is useful to talk about something you know well—this allows your focus to go toward practicing eye contact rather than thinking hard about what to say next.
- As you speak, focus solely on keeping eye contact with one participant at a time. Fully complete one sentence or thought (which could be more than one sentence) with that participant, then move your eye contact to another participant.
- Clearly establish eye contact with this second participant before you begin a new sentence. Again, complete a full sentence or thought with that participant.
- Move your eye contact to the third participant before you begin another sentence or thought. Keep repeating this pattern of sustained eye contact throughout the three minutes.

- When your three minutes are over, pause for a quick self-observation: How did you do with this skill practice? What went well? What could be improved?
- Elicit feedback from your audience. How did they feel about the eye contact they received from you? What did you do well? What might enhance your use of eye contact?
- Repeat the exercise twice more, this time speaking for only two minutes at a time. Remember—the focus of the exercise is not to entertain your friends with your stories.
- Repeat the feedback process after each round. Always offer your own feedback first, then listen to the feedback from your audience. And end the ten-minute practice session with an assessment of your strengths in the skill you practiced, as well as any insights on how you would like to further develop your mastery of this skill.
- I urge you to stick to the same content in each of the three practice rounds. This will help you and your audience stay focused on the skill you are practicing: sustaining eye contact one sentence, or one thought, at a time.

Exercise 2: Holding Eye Contact When You Don't Know What to Say

The purpose of this exercise is to catch the involuntary eye movements that happen when we don't know what to say next—those moments when we want to stare into outer space, at the floor, our shoes, our wrists. The eye movements are often just a quick flicker, and they are the sort of movements that many of us are entirely unaware of. The feedback from your participants will, thus, be especially crucial in this exercise. They will notice the involuntary movements that, quite literally, escape you.

- As you did in Exercise 1, speak freely for three minutes on a topic you know well. Your inner focus as you speak is to stay fully connected through eye contact in all of those moments when you don't know what to say next.

- Hold eye contact with one of your three audience members at all times—for the entire three minutes of your speech. Don't ever lose this eye-to-eye connection.
- Notice the moments when your eyes want to wander, when the words or thoughts are not freely coming to you, and commit to staying connected with a participant through eye contact.
- After three minutes, pause for a quick self-observation: How did you do with this skill practice? What went well? What could be improved?
- Elicit feedback from your audience. What did you do well? Were there any moments when your eyes lost focus? What sort of involuntary eye movements occurred that you may not have noticed?
- Repeat the exercise twice more, this time only speaking for two minutes at a time.
- Repeat the feedback process after each round. Always offer your own feedback first, then listen to the feedback from your audience. And end the ten-minute practice session with an assessment of your strengths in the skill you practiced, as well as any insights on how you would like to further develop your mastery of this skill.

Exercise 3: Creating Eye Contact in the Face of Resistance

Creating sustained eye contact can be challenging enough when we talk to an audience that is giving us undivided attention. It can be an even more daunting task when we address a group that is distracted, not interested in what we have to say, or restless and not offering eye contact in return. Frequently, our first instinct is to not attempt to generate any eye contact at all.

I'm not proposing we make eye contact with an audience member at all cost, even when he is clearly sending us hostile energy. But quite often the individual who is not offering us eye contact will sense strongly that *we* are sending eye contact and are seeking his eye response. Our intentional eye contact can be the cue that brings him back to the room, the presentation, and, yes, the eyes of the presenter.

The purpose of this exercise, then, is to seek and generate eye contact even when a participant is not looking at us.

- Ask each of your three helpers to pick a specific nonverbal activity that she or he is engaged in as you begin your three-minute speech. For example—doodling in a notebook, playing with a pen, fiddling with her hair, looking through his wallet, adjusting a piece of clothing.
- Let them know that they are giving you what I will term a "mid-level of resistance." "Mid-level" quite simply means that they are engaged in their activity but, if they sense your eye contact strongly enough, may be willing to redirect their attention to you.
- As you speak, continuously seek to generate eye contact with your audience members, even though none of them may initially be returning your gaze.
- This exercise may bring up strong feelings. Observe the feelings that arise for you, and notice how they impact your progress through the three-minute presentation. Our feelings, notably resentment or frustration with participants who are not fully present, will affect our desire to use eye contact.
- When your three minutes are over, pause for a quick self-observation: How did you do with this skill practice? How did you channel the feelings that arose? Did they become a barrier to the communication process? Or did they motivate you to seek eye contact with added fervor?
- Listen to feedback from your participants. Did they sense your eye contact? Was it strong enough to pull them away from their preoccupations?
- Repeat the exercise twice more, this time only speaking for two minutes at a time.
- Repeat the feedback process after each round. Offer your own feedback first, then listen to the feedback from your audience. And end the ten-minute practice session with an assessment of your strengths in the skill you practiced, as well as any insights on how you would like to further develop your mastery of this skill.

CHAPTER 5

Energy

My colleague, Alisa Alexander, is a sparkling jewel on the speaking circuit. A sought-after keynote speaker and master trainer, Alisa doesn't merely get up in front of a group to talk. Alisa holds court. She glitters and shines. Alisa is a diva.

The first time I watched Alisa speak in front of a group, it was clear that her energy touched and enthralled everyone in the room. During a break in the seminar, I walked up to her to have a private chat. I noticed that her hand was clutching a stool, and I was surprised by how weak she suddenly seemed. Tired, almost frail. "Oh Lord," Alisa said to me, "I'm so exhausted from being on the road, and I'm having problems with my knees after this knee surgery I had. I just want to go lie down and go to bed."

That's when Alisa climbed yet another notch on my admiration scale. Even though she was having a difficult day, Alisa knew how to dig down deep and harness whatever reservoirs of personal energy she could summon to engage her audience. The audience clearly had no idea that Alisa was not feeling well. So how was Alisa able to pull forth all of this energy when it clearly wasn't her day?

"Fake it till you feel it," was her answer when I inquired.

Alisa said this somewhat tongue-in-cheek, but I was delighted that she used the verb "fake." Alisa wasn't recommending that we "be fake" or "act fake." No, she clearly meant that even though we may not feel energetic, by acting as if we are we will actually begin to access some of the hidden reserves of energy that are tucked away inside of us.

Let us toy for a moment with the words "energy" and "fake." Many of my clients like to associate a more energetic presentation style with being fake or phony. This perception harks back to the adjective we explored in the previous chapter: Being more energetic doesn't feel *natural*. Being low-key and restrained does. Problem is, we take what is comfortable for us in a one-on-one encounter and expect to have the same sensation in a public environment where we are the focal point of everyone's attention. The moment we speak in public, however, we are in a relationship with more than one other person. It, quite simply, takes a little more energy to sustain this relationship with a collection of individuals. And as the speaker, we need to learn how to draw from our inner energy well.

Alisa put it this way for me: "When I speak in front of people, I'm the Energizer Bunny."

I think of my lessons as an actor when I contemplate Alisa's phrase. One slogan that I picked up early on has stuck with me ever since: "Play to the last row." Make sure every member of your audience receives your energy. Or, to evoke a phrase from the world of group processing and group dynamics: Use your energy to "hold the space" for everyone in the audience. The challenge for the speaker with a large audience is not at all unlike that of an actor in a larger theater. How do I project a larger sense of myself without becoming "fake?" How do I enlarge and expand my presence and still feel like I am myself? The stereotype about actors is that they are always "on." They seem just a little too dramatic. Too "actory." Too fake.

What associations come to mind when you hear the word "energy"? Do you think of the kind of manic energy that manifests when people are intoxicated? Or the frantic energy of the compulsive personality who seems "out of control?" The almost desperate energy of the class clown who will stop at nothing to get attention? I'm thinking more of the sort of pure, clear, focused energy that comes from very deep within us.

I like the way my colleague, Clare Maxwell, refers to energy. A choreographer and certified teacher of the Alexander Technique in New York City, she explains it as follows: "Westerners always think they have to do more, more, more. They see themselves as causative agents for everything. If they don't *do* something, they think that nothing will happen. Truth is, we can access greater energy by getting out of the way, doing less, and letting the true energy that is already there come out."

And how exactly do we get out of our own way? "We have to stop interfering with our natural energy resources," Clare explains. "So first we need to simply become aware of all the things we do to block energy from being released through us. Everyone has a kinetic sense, but my clients who are the most blocked are often least able to access that sense. They don't know how their bodies feel."

Which takes us right back to the elusive and liberating state of self-awareness that we visited earlier in the book. While our bodies are designed for freedom and balance, many of us keep our bodies in rigid holding patterns. Some people's bodies are too flaccid. These folks have to learn to become energized and excited; they need the experience of vital movement. Other people have bodies that work way too hard to simply stand up; they need to discover the use of their joints. Some people physically remove their muscles from the ground every time they get scared; they need to learn how to rely on the support of the earth.

These are just a few of the ways in which we shut our bodies down. If we can't sense these ways in which we interfere with ourselves, then our bodies won't give up the interference. The Alexander Technique uses the term "inhibition," or *non-doing*, to refer to our nervous system's ability to rebalance itself when in a state of excitement. Inhibition is not a psychological term but a physiological one. All of us have this capacity to get quiet and focused. Instead of holding back we can pause, notice if we *are* holding back, and choose to undo that holding. This undoing unleashes our hidden energy and allows us powerful new choices in the moment.

The first time we allow a larger energy to move through us, it will feel unfamiliar. A little terrifying, perhaps. Certainly unknown. "Body awareness," Clare declares emphatically, "is about leaving the terrible prison of habit." Behind the prison walls lurk tremendous reservoirs of energy that we have not utilized. I'm not partial to the corporate pet phrase of "think out of the box," but it certainly applies to the new ways in which we will need to access and channel our personal energy. Hand in hand with our physical inhibitors, most of us have also learned to "play small" in every other aspect of life. Well, the very act of public speaking requires that we draw attention. Like it or not, for that span of time when we share a space with an audience, we are the center of attention. Every one of us makes choices about the manner in which we claim this center. But regardless of the degree to which we bask in the spotlight, every act of public speaking inherently requires us to jump over our own shadow.

I appreciate the presenter who is willing to make this an energetic jump. My willingness to be energetic sends many implicit messages to my audience. Energy says I value you as an audience member. I take you seriously. I don't wish to bore you. No, my intent is to engage, excite, stimulate, and motivate you. I'm willing to put out all the stops for you.

This is the promise of a more energetic delivery style: You will have more fun as you speak. Your audience will have more fun. You will actually feel less nervous, because your nervousness will be transformed into energy (and we're not talking about a nervously scattered energy). I am closing this first section of *Power Speaking* with an exploration of personal energy, because I trust that it will now be an energy that is supported by a strong voice, by a balance between stillness and purposeful movement, by fluid gestures, and by sustained eye contact. Put all of this together, and you have already become a channel for focused energy.

What will prevent you from crossing the line and turning into the manic Energizer Bunny on speed? The sort of presenter who seems to assault the audience with his energy? That presenter is invariably doing all of the energy work on his own, without responding to, or receiving, the energy of his audience. Energy is fluid. It has velocity and direction. And it is cyclical. We generate energy when we speak, send it out, and then we let the energy that is sent back to us come in as well. Energy that exists in a vacuum, without reciprocal flow, is blocked energy. Such one-directional energy actually becomes another inhibitor: it prevents a relationship with the audience.

This relationship will be the main focus of the second part of *Power Speaking*. In part II, we will move beyond our exploration of the basic communication instruments and begin to take a look at all of the ways in which we shape, and surrender to, this relationship with our audience.

PRACTICE EXERCISES

To help you explore how you channel and experience energy, you will undertake two very different kinds of exercises. In the first of these exercises, you will spend some time by yourself, moving through space and consciously sensing energy within your body. In the second exercise, you will once again invite a group of three friends or colleagues to give you feedback. Through the use of an imaginary "energy-meter," you will have the opportunity to modulate and shift energy; your friends, in turn, will let you know how they experience your energy levels.

Exercise 1: Personal Energy Exploration

We can have powerful experiences of energy in moments of stillness, but often energy is stirred up and unleashed as we move about. I want to give you a strong sense of how exhilarating it can be to feel energy pulsing through your body. Many of us remember peak moments in our lives—moments of joy, exhilaration, accomplishment, abandonment—when the sense of energy within us was indeed palpable. We could "feel" our energy. Wouldn't it be nice if we could intentionally re-create those vibrant states of energy, instead of waiting for those moments of divine intervention when they seem to manifest themselves of their own accord?

To help you reconnect with those powerful states of energy flowing through your body, I ask you to find a place where you can freely move about, unobserved. A public park space when there is nobody around, an empty parking lot or alley, the garden of your house, an empty gym, a beach during off-hours—any of these would be terrific environments for conducting your personal energy exercise. During your movement exploration, you will execute typical children's movements that we all have engaged in at one point or other in our lives: skipping, hopping, jumping, leaping, rolling on the ground. You may have others of your own. I invite you to perform these children's movements because, quite simply, when we were young many of us tended to perform them with great joy and abandonment. We relished the energy that these movements generated within us. And they were simple, easy movements. They didn't require any hard work. But they made us feel amazing—and they helped uncork our energy.

As grown-ups, it's not too "cool" to engage in these movements in public. You probably don't skip down the parking lot as you head from your car to your office. It wouldn't look very businesslike. Well, this exercise is not about being businesslike. No, we want to reconnect with those boundless states of energy that we have all known, and that we have abandoned for the sake of more proper (and energyless) behavior. Are we going to skip and jump around as we speak in public? Not likely. But we certainly want to be able to access this energy that we all have inside of us. It's infectious. And it's the source that will inform any topic, anywhere, anytime that we present.

- Get yourself to that public space where you have planned to conduct your movement exploration. It will be helpful if you are alone. This will encourage you to move freely without worrying about what an onlooker might think.
- Before you begin, you may wish to decide what movements you want to explore. Will this be your jumping exploration? Or your skipping exploration? Chances are your movement choices will evolve and change anyway, but it will help give you a point of departure.

- Remember—there is no way of "doing this wrong" or "messing up." When you start moving about, simply surrender to executing these movements. If it is skipping, skip with commitment. Skip full out. Skip high. Skip quickly. Skip slowly. As you skip, feel the way your body slices through space. And feel the energy that is released within you by your skips.

- There is no time limit to this movement exploration. You'll know when you're running out of steam, or out of breath. Your body will tell you; you won't have to decide.

- When you find yourself winding down, come to a moment of stillness and stand in that still place for a while. Breathe and notice how powerfully you are breathing. Above all, sense the energy that is moving through your body. It may help you to close your eyes. With all external distractions banished, notice what happens to your body when energy is coursing through it. And if there are parts of your body that feel tense or constricted, notice that as well. Your body is a channel for your personal energy, and you want to know what happens inside of it when energy gets activated.

- Indulge yourself in at least one or two more movement explorations. Again, it may help you to first select the movement you wish to explore. Will this be your hopping exploration? Or the leaping one? Once you begin, surrender fully to these movements. Allow them to evolve into other movements if that is what they want to do. Explore these movements in all of their facets—vary your speed, your level, your direction. Notice what it feels like to be inside of your body as you commit to these motions. Observe the energy that is moving through your body as you move through space.

- After each movement exploration, find the moment of stillness again. Close your eyes. Notice how you experience the energy that has been stirred up within you.

- When your body has decided that is has moved enough, you may wish to sit or lie down for a moment and pull out a notebook. Many of the exercises in this book aim to help you experience your instrument (i.e., yourself) in a different way. And along the way, you will develop an awareness of what happens inside of you as you move and speak. Awareness is the great beginning point for doing things differently.

- So, as you unwind, contemplate the following two questions in your notebook:
  - How and where in my body do I experience energy?
  - What are the places in my body where I block or inhibit energy?

Exercise 2: Energy Meter

Gather three friends or colleagues around you for an opportunity to play with raising or lowering your energy levels as you speak. Let your friends know that they will be your energy barometer. They can stop you at any point during your presentation to ask you to climb higher or drop lower on your personal energy scale. When they stop you during your presentation, they must give you a specific energy goal. It is simplest to state this goal in percentages. For example, I might stop you and say: "Give us 30 percent more." When you continue, you will try to get a sense of what it feels like to raise your energy level by 30 percent. If your friends are not satisfied that you have sufficiently elevated your energy, they may stop you again and side-coach some more: "That was 20 percent, now bring it up to 30." Or if they are satisfied, they may want to nudge you a little further: "That was great—now give us another 20 percent."

As you have done in previous practice rounds with an audience, keep the exercise to roughly ten minutes. The purpose of this exercise is to get a sense of what it feels like to you, the speaker, as you summon more energy or lower your energy output. You will learn that you are quite capable of calling upon energy levels that you frequently do not use. I do not propose that every presentation should be delivered at a very high energy level—the level of energy required will always be influenced by the setting, the size of the audience, and the nature of your topic. This activity is intended as a simple confidence builder—I want you to know, and experience, the different energy states that you are able to access as you speak.

- Pick a topic that you can comfortably talk about for three minutes. Make sure your audience members know that it is their job to stop you during your presentation and provide you with energy goals.
- As you receive coaching, tap into your inner energy meter and raise or drop your energy levels. Stay open to all of the coaching you receive, even if what you are asked to do feels uncomfortable or like a bit of a stretch—that is the purpose of the exercise.
- Embrace the moments of discomfort—if you walk through those moments, you are likely to find a liberating new sense of energy directly afterward. What you are asked to do feels?
- When your three minutes are over, pause for a quick self-observation: How did you do with this skill practice? What went well? What could be improved?
- Elicit feedback from your audience. Did they feel that you were able to raise or lower your energy levels to match the coaching they gave you? What was their overall sense of your energy level? Was it just right? Too low? Too over the top? How did they experience the energy they received from you?
- Repeat the exercise once or twice more, this time speaking for only two minutes at a time. Before you start each new round, ask your audience members to get you started with an energy goal. Again, encourage them to side-coach you as they see fit. Remind them that it is their job to nudge you beyond your "energy comfort zone" and help you experience new ways of channeling energy while you speak.
- Repeat the feedback process after each round. Always offer your own feedback first, then listen to the feedback from your audience. And end the ten-minute practice session with an assessment of your strengths in the skill you practiced, as well as any insights on how you would like to further develop your mastery of this skill.

The Art of the Connection

PART II

This is how my audiences describe their ideal speaker:
"We want someone who is *dynamic!*" Well, how do I suddenly, magically transform myself into a dynamic speaker? Do I go to dynamism boot camp? Do I press some invisible button and suddenly tap into my dynamic gene? Or is this dynamic quality one of those gifts that one speaker always has in abundance while it forever eludes another?

In part I, we looked at the basic tools of the public speaker—what actors tend to call the "instrument." An ease and comfort level with these tools takes every speaker a little bit of the way toward becoming that dynamic presenter the audience craves. But it is nearly impossible to be dynamic all on our own. The word "dynamic" suggests flexibility and fluidity. And the text of a speech will seldom provide all of this fluidity for us. No, the variable that is new and fluid in every presentation is the audience. The dynamic qualities of a presentation emerge the moment we truly engage with this audience. So, while part I was squarely concerned with the instrument, part II will explore the shared process between speaker and audience. We will investigate the communication tools that help us to engage our audience. And we will look at how we play with the signals the audience sends us in return. This back and forth between audience and speaker, and the continual process of engagement and re-engagement, leads us to the goal of this part of *Power Speaking*: to create a connection.

Here's where we begin to separate the beginner from the advanced presenter. A novice speaker tends to focus on "doing things right." He is primarily concerned with his performance. He worries about all of the tools we discussed in part I of this book. He wants to make sure that nothing goes wrong. The advanced speaker trusts that the tools are there to support the far more important part of his presentation—his relationship with his audience. His focus goes entirely away from himself. He is intent on engaging, motivating, inspiring, and challenging his audience. He notices, moment by moment, what is happening in the presentation environment. He responds to the signals and messages he receives from his audience. He changes and adapts his presentation on the fly. He is singularly intent on creating the connection.

Is this easy to do? No. But the answers to many of the dilemmas that arise for every speaker—dilemmas such as "How do I keep my presentation fresh?"—can be found in this section. A relationship is always fresh, because it lives and breathes in every new moment that unfolds. Can this be dangerous? Sure. Risky? Yes. But my focus on this relationship also promises aliveness and likely inspiration. The moment I give myself to this relationship, no presentation will ever be exactly like the previous one. That may be the very thing I fear. But it is also the beauty and the essence of this relationship approach to speaking. It takes me right into the unpredictable mystery of what happens when people congregate. I don't believe there is any other way.

The second I shift my focus from what I do and how well I do it to how the audience responds, I have started to engage in a whole new dance. I no longer have to lead with every step. I will quite often be led and guided by my partner. Suddenly, there is no such thing as a bad dance. Now, I may like some dance partners better than others. There will be dances that I will wish never to end. And there will be those where I can't wait for the music to stop. But every dance will just be what it is—a new dance with a new partner. A dance that has never unfolded exactly the way it is unfolding, in the very moment when I am "doing the dancing."

Since we're toying with the word "power" and its many implications in this book, please note that we're not entirely powerless over the nature of this dance. As the speaker, we are invariably the official focal point of the dance event. So, the tools discussed in this section are, very simply, the little ways in which we influence the nature of this event. A spicy story can turn our dance into a samba. A reflective story can turn it into a languid waltz. A provocative question can initiate a never-ending line dance. A humorous reflection may send your audience into a quick and wild, quirky dance improvisation. Within one presentation, many different dances will happen. And they will happen spontaneously, because every dance partner offers a new step, new mood, new variation, new possibilities.

There are very tangible ways in which we help to shape these possibilities. In the upcoming chapters, we will look at the role of a speaker's intent. How do you wish to affect your audience? What kind of impact do you want to evoke? We will examine ways of creating a poignant and well-placed thematic frame for our content. We will look at how we use humor to put an audience at ease, and we will have the opportunity to identify a humor style that works for us. We will explore the benefits of turning a monologue into a dialogue, through the use of classic questioning and listening tools. And we will clarify ways of working with, and transforming, a resistant audience.

I hope the message of this introduction is blazingly clear: Even a resistant audience is not a "bad" audience. There really, truly is no such thing as a *bad* speaking event. The moment we accept this basic premise, we're already halfway down the path to speaker liberation. Accepting this premise allows us to remain open to the ever-present possibility of connection, regardless of the particular dynamics of a certain group of individuals. The dance is always just the dance. The tools in this section will help us to subtly shift each dance into a truly engaging one.

CHAPTER 6

Finding the Intention

I spent my childhood traveling in foreign countries. There were many times when my parents and I found ourselves staring at a map, trying to decide how we could best get to a destination we had never visited before. The map would always show us that there was more than one way to reach our destination. Multiple roads could eventually get us there. Some looked shorter, others longer. But one or two were likely full of snarled traffic. Others were just as likely bumpy, potholed, or entirely impassable. And some, we always hoped, would be expedient and direct.

Often, speaking in front of an audience we have never met is like traveling into a foreign country. We don't quite know what the end of the road into this country will look like. But here is where the beauty and the power of conscious intention come into play: A speaker's intention will always charge the most direct path to its unfamiliar destination. Intention adds a sense of urgency to the journey. Not only does it cause expediency, it also tends to generate a measure of excitement and engagement along the way. Conscious intention is as close as we ever get to a guarantee that we will successfully reach "the end."

As we contemplate ways of speaking with intention, we continue from exactly where we left off in the previous section of this book. For, more than anything else, our intention will single-handedly harness, shape, and direct our energy. A strong intention can pull energy from within us that we didn't know we had. It will focus this energy in a clear and direct manner. And it will, of course, energize the audience, even if that is not its primary goal.

Having a clear intention is also another way of saying, "Hey, I care about my audience." We have all listened to the speaker who seems to be grandstanding. Everything this speaker says and does seems to scream, "Look how fabulous I am!" He just loves the sound of his voice. Speaking in public is his way of stroking his insatiable ego. Well, choosing a clear intention is the first step in shifting the attention away from me, the speaker, to you, the audience. Suddenly, the way in which I hope to impact you, my audience, becomes a good deal more important than the way in which I deliver my content. Everything I do will synergistically place itself in the service of this intention. Everything will begin to align with my clear purpose for speaking.

How do I select an intention? How do I know that I have an intention that is powerful and that "works"? The best intentions are simple, clear action verbs that describe in one word the impact I wish to have on my audience. Here is my personal top-ten list of compelling intentions. This is by no means an exhaustive list, but these are classic intentions that often come into play when a speaker seeks to fully reach an audience. You will note that the action verbs do not describe what I, the speaker, *do*—they solely describe my desired impact on the audience.

With this presentation, I want to . . .

- *Move* my audience
- *Motivate* my audience
- *Challenge* my audience
- *Provoke* my audience
- *Enchant* my audience
- *Inspire* my audience
- *Persuade* my audience
- *Transform* my audience
- *Entertain* my audience
- *Calm* my audience

As you play with selecting strong action verbs, you will find that some work better for you than others. How do you know that you have chosen a "workable" intention? Well, here's a quick intention test for you. The best intention verbs are verbs that speak to you, the speaker, as well. You "get" what these verbs are all about. You get them on a visceral, kinesthetic level. They make you tingle. They excite you. They get you going. They turn you on. What a great starting point for a presentation! And chances are, if you are turned on by your intention, the audience will be turned on too.

Actors work with strong intentions—or as they call them, "objectives"—all the time. They quickly learn the difference between "real life," where folks often operate without a real or conscious objective, and the world of stage and screen, where time is much more finite and condensed. To help shape this finite time, every moment of an actor's work is guided by the choice of provocative objectives. For a great example of objective-driven screen acting, I urge you to watch Susan Sarandon's Oscar-winning performance in *Dead Man Walking*. The beauty of her performance lies in its unflinching focus. Shot by shot, there is a clear purpose to everything she does. There is not a superfluous gesture, movement, expression, none of what we call "mugging" or "milking" or "overworking the moment"—the trademarks of a less-skilled actor. No, Sarandon's work is efficient, spare, and directed.

That's the power of clear intention.

And you will note that Sarandon doesn't need to state her intention—frame by frame, we get what her intention is! When speaking in public, we sometimes hear a speaker state the goal or purpose of a meeting as he begins to speak. Fine. That's what I call the "external" or "official" objective. It will rarely generate a lot of excitement in the listener. But just as Sarandon does not declare her character's inner objectives to the viewer, I urge speakers not to reveal those inner intentions we will be exploring in this chapter. Instead, *focus* on the inner intention, and focus on it with full commitment. The audience will receive the emotional impact of the intention. Guaranteed.

Much like in acting, a speaker's presentation does not have to be limited to one intention. There will always be the main intention, which I like to call the "through line" of the speech. The through line is my inner reason for giving the speech. I may, for example, wish to motivate, to excite, or to entertain the audience. But there can be multiple segments within a presentation, which actors call "beats," and different beats or segments can have sub-intentions to support the main intention. For example, even though my through line may be to entertain my audience, there can be segments in which I seek to provoke folks, move folks, startle folks. The beauty of clear intentions is that we don't need to understand the mysteries of how they work. They simply do. They channel, mold, and shape our message in ways we cannot consciously manipulate. A clear intention becomes the wonderful connector between all the thoughts and emotions we wish to convey, and the way in which the audience receives those very thoughts and emotions.

In this section, I invite you to play with strong intentions. Choose action verbs that stimulate you. Think and fully claim the intentions, and you will be surprised by what they pull from within you. And, above all, I urge you not to second-guess the process. It works in wondrous ways that we do not need to understand!

PRACTICE EXERCISE

In preparation for this practice, select two or three short texts that you will use as a basis for exploring the impact of intentions. For the purpose of this exercise, it will be most beneficial if they are texts that you have memorized. When we improvise and speak spontaneously, our attention will often go toward finding the next thought or the right word, at the expense of focusing on our intention. You may wish to use one of the texts you used for the exercises in the chapter on voice (chapter 1), or you may choose a section of a speech that you have to deliver in a professional environment.

Next, for each text select three action verbs that will serve as the intentions for your exploration. Make sure you select action verbs that seek to create a variety of different impacts on your audience. Remember—the same text can be used to both move and motivate an audience. You want to have the opportunity to experience how a radically different choice of intention creates a radically different impact on your audience, and also how it taps into different energies within you. It can be great fun to pull out a thesaurus and explore different choices of language. You may wish to write down all the verbs that, for whatever reason, tickle your fancy—verbs that surprise you, verbs that are bold, verbs that are literate, verbs that contain energy simply because of the sounds they contain. Remember—select action verbs that speak to you, stimulate you, and get you excited!

Now you're ready to begin:

- As you have done in previous practice exercises, gather a group of three friends or colleagues around you. It is certainly possible to practice intentions with just one audience member, but a larger audience will usually demand a stronger energy release with your intention. Furthermore, validation and feedback from a group of three is always likely to be more objective than the feedback of one.
- Limit each exercise to a length of ten minutes. A ten-minute time limit gives a manageable focus to each exercise, and it will help everyone stay on task.
- Make sure everyone understands the purpose of the exercise. Let your friends know that you are practicing the use of strong focus and intention. Do not, however, tell them which specific intentions you are planning to explore in your practice. This conversation will be part of the debriefing with your audience.
- Select only one of your prepared pieces for this exercise. Speak for only two minutes, even if this piece is longer. Make sure one of your audience members keeps track of the time for you. While you speak, put all of your attention on the impact you wish to have on your audience—the impact that is articulated by your intention.
- When you stop, debrief and ask your audience members how they feel after having listened to your presentation. Remember that you are not seeking feedback on the particular details of what you said. An intention seeks to create an emotional response in your audience, so it is imperative that they communicate what, if any, emotional response they have after listening to you.

- If your audience clearly received your intention—i.e., you wished to excite your audience members, and they all stated that they did feel excited by your presentation, great! Let them know that this was indeed your intention.
- Proceed and present the same text again, this time focusing on a different intention. Notice how the same text can feel entirely different with a new intention. Notice how it will elicit new energies, new phrasing, new emphasis, new movement and gestures from you, simply because you are choosing to focus on a different intention.
- If during your first practice round your audience members did not "get" your intention, let them know what your intention was. Present the text again, focusing on the same intention. Let them know that you are seeking to convey the same intention more strongly this time.
- After your second practice round—whether it involved a new intention or the one from your first round—ask your audience members, once again, to tell you how your presentation affected them. Make sure they respond by giving you a "feeling description," not an intellectual analysis of your speech.
- If audience members have suggestions for you about how you can better actualize your intention, great! Beware, however, of feedback that focuses purely on the outer mechanics of presenting—i.e., more movement, more volume, more gestures, etc. A strong intention is always an inside job, and your unwavering inner focus on the intention will, in turn, begin to change all of the outer mechanics your audience gets to witness.
- If time permits, present the same text a third time. Select a different intention and then repeat the feedback process from the two preceding rounds.
- End the ten-minute practice session with an assessment of your strengths in the skill you practiced, as well as any insights on how you would like to further develop your mastery of this skill. Resist the temptation to use all of your texts in one practice round. The power of this exercise lies in the repetition of the same text with different intentions. Save another text for another practice round.

CHAPTER 7

Selecting the Frame

From the moment we start to speak, every word we utter helps to create a framework for how our audience experiences the content or message of our presentation. Framing, and the way we frame and reframe content, is one of the truly simple yet infinitely powerful ways in which we engage people. Some of my colleagues like to call this process the "positioning of content." Others refer to it as "creating the hook." Both of these terms originate in the world of advertising and marketing. I like them, but the concept of creating frames has infinitely broader implications and possibilities. A hook seeks to quickly stimulate and excite an audience. A frame, on the other hand, shapes and focuses an entire presentation; it creates resonance and helps the listener forge a personal connection to the content.

Any topic I present can be contained by more than one frame. The frame, much like the view through a camera lens, can have a narrow or a wide angle. It shapes and manages the viewing field of the audience, and becomes the context that creates clarity, focus, and hopefully understanding. Frames are not rigid—we can change a frame to help create a new perspective. Frames create lucidity. They shape perception. Above all, they stimulate and engage.

Let's take a topic that is personal to me: the events of 9/11 in New York City. I was living in Manhattan's West Village at the time, a good half-hour walk from the World Trade Center. There are many different ways of talking about an event of such magnitude. One frame is the loss of innocent life in a terrorist attack. Another frame is the bravery of the New York City police officers and firefighters. Another is the loss of an individual's sense of safety and security. Yet another is the experience of non-Americans like me at a time of great patriotic expression. The reassessment of our relationship to home, and what home is. The reaction of the rest of the world to this attack. The ways in which trauma manifests in the body. . . . The list of potential frames goes on and on, yet each frame plays off one central event.

A story is not the only way to create a frame, but it is a compelling way to do so. Later in this chapter, we'll look a little more closely at the ways we tell stories. But a pertinent statistic, a quote from a magazine, an accessible analogy, a compelling visual aid, a quick demonstration—they all can serve as a quick framing device that engages our audience and focuses the presentation. If I were to speak about what happened on 9/11, I might rely a good deal on stories, since I was in New York when the events unfurled. For the loss of life frame, for example, I might speak about the experience of walking through Union Square Park just days after the attack, surrounded by the hundreds of impromptu memorials that cropped up. For the bravery of the police and firemen frame, I might talk of the experience of standing on New York's West Side Highway to cheer on the thousands of helpers that were racing toward Ground Zero to help the wounded and search for survivors. For the loss of personal safety frame, I might talk of listening for days on end to the sirens of emergency vehicles as they raced past my house, and smelling the stench that wafted from the Trade Center site toward my neighborhood.

Are you still not sure of the importance of a frame? Here's a high-stakes situation from my conflict-resolution life, where my choice of the frame consistently determines the difference between success and failure. Once or twice a year for nearly a decade, I have facilitated international dialogue projects between Israelis and Palestinians. I'm hired to guide the conversation between parties on two sides of a political conflict, with divergent views of history and very strong feelings about the circumstances under which they live. The first event in such a project is always the introduction, where both participants and I get to tell about ourselves. A classic simple speaking event. Sounds innocent enough, doesn't it?

When I have conducted introductions without a frame, participants tend to vacillate between cool and formal introductions that don't reveal anything personal at all and prepared political grandstanding that is intended to incite. I, on the other hand, am interested in fostering an environment in which everyone can truly see and hear those who are present, regardless of where they come from. So I have learned to put a simple symbolic frame on the introductions: we play with the idea that every one of us wears invisible lenses that color the way we view the world.

Every participant draws large eyeglass frames on a piece of flipchart paper. I present seven specific questions that allow participants to explain what they value about key aspects of their lives—questions about their families, their home, their religion, their heroes, their leisure activities. The answer to each question is drawn with crayons inside of the eyeglasses as a symbolic representation of the things that matter to each individual.

Now we conduct the introductions.

One by one, participants present their prepared eyeglasses to the group and narrate the answers they drew inside their lenses. Invariably, this telling is very poignant and moving. Participants are able to see what they have in common and also able to hear their differences. Frequently, it reduces those present to tears. And the power of this entire introduction is shaped solely by the choice of the frame.

What makes the eyeglasses a powerful frame? Well, it has several dimensions that help create resonance: The use of eyeglasses as a metaphor for how we view the world allows for both commonality and individuality. The use of seven key questions that everyone answers again generates both common ground and individuality. The use of crayons to draw the answers creates an atmosphere of childlike innocence and vulnerability. The narrating of the lenses allows for an honest, emotionally truthful, and purposeful introduction to the speaker.

THREE LANGUAGE FRAMES

I don't analyze every frame according to such dimensions. At some point, I simply start to play with frames and note the impact they have on an audience. But I have learned that every single word I speak will influence the way the relationship with my audience unfolds. The very language I choose, from the moment I begin to address my audience, creates a context for the entire speaking event. It sends implicit messages about how I view this relationship with my audience members. Coaching corporate trainers, who on a daily basis speak in public, has made me hyperconscious of the power of the unintended verbal cue. Here, for example, are three key language frames that come into play when we address an audience: the "dictator frame," the "group frame," and the "invitational frame."

The dictator frame puts an inordinate emphasis on the authority of the speaker. "I want you to" is the favorite phrase used by the speaker who operates within this frame. The choice of language emphasizes the power the speaker perceives she has over an audience. It can be a useful frame if the intent is to consistently remind the audience "who's the boss." Chances are, however, that the audience will have mental associations with past schoolteachers, temperamental preachers, or tough parents, and all of their ambivalent feelings about these relationships will be played out within this frame.

The group frame places a good deal of emphasis on the experience of the group as a whole. "Let's look at this for a moment" or "We'll take a few minutes to explore" or "Why don't we see what else we can do" are some of the ways in which the speaker will address her audience in this frame. She intentionally chooses language that makes her a part of the audience. "We," "us," and "together" are key words in the group frame. The speaker's language makes her "one of the gang" and minimizes her place as the expert, the authority figure, or the center of attention. The group frame tends to be an inclusive frame that helps create a measure of comfort for the audience. There will, however, be audiences who don't want the speaker to be "one of the gang." They want the speaker to claim the mantle of the expert, with a stronger emphasis on "I-language" rather than "we-language."

In the invitational frame, the speaker relies on language that is more allusive and descriptive, and allows the listener to fill in the details with his feelings and personal associations. Imagine, for a moment, that you are sitting in a theater and you're about to see a play. If you're in a big Broadway theater, there's a good chance that the moment the curtain rises, you will see a lavishly produced, highly elaborate, very detailed, and boldly lit stage set. It will elicit applause the moment the curtain goes up. It has been designed to do just that. If the setting is a mansion, for example, every little detail of the mansion will be painstakingly rendered and shown. It will likely be a quite spectacular mansion—and it will also leave very little room for your imagination.

In a simpler theater that has less of a budget for opulent set design, you might encounter a more minimalist, evocative set. A few windows, a door, a hanging lamp—they will be the few and only set pieces that, taken together, evoke the presence of a vast mansion. Thus, not all of the particulars of this mansion are revealed to the audience. The set merely creates an environmental hint or guideline, and the actual details will be brought to life by the audience's imagination.

The invitational frame is the speaking equivalent of the minimalist set. "Imagine" is the choice verb in this invitational frame. I invite audience members to participate in my presentation by offering key words, concepts, ideas. I paint a picture that helps to evoke the memories and personal associations of my audience. The invitational frame is inherently a connecting and engaging frame, not a "feeding" frame. A feeding frame spells everything out for the audience. It is the equivalent of running into an "all-you-can-eat" restaurant and trying to eat as much food as you can in ten minutes or less. Chances are a lot of food will pass through your mouth, yet you won't remember what any of it tastes like. The invitational frame, on the other hand, stimulates an audience's mind and senses. It does not feed them all of the details—on the contrary, meaning emerges only if they actively chew, imbibe, savor, and digest all the little nuggets and morsels they are served.

Stories are a very potent part of this invitational frame. They humanize and personalize seemingly dry or lifeless content. They give the audience the opportunity to connect with the speaker's vulnerability, which in turn stirs their vulnerability as well. The best stories have a beautiful way of tapping into both an audience's hearts and minds. They take us back to the roots of how people, throughout history, have found meaning and made sense of the world. They connect us with the little child who had stories read to him in bed, or the teenager who told stories around the campfire, or (if you've never had any of those experiences) the part of you that always longed to have a story told to you. A story is the most universal, timeless, ageless, and unifying way to engage an audience.

STORYTELLING

Is it easy to tell a story? Sure. There are three guidelines we need to remember when telling a story to an audience:

Guideline #1: Know why you're telling the story, and the point this story seeks to highlight.

Guideline #2: Don't dwell on the exposition or background for long; get into the story quickly.

Guideline #3: Remember that old adage "Show, don't tell"? Well, when it comes to storytelling, the adage is "Tell, don't telegraph." Quite simply, have the courage to really tell the story by taking the audience into the experience, rather than "telegraphing" the message. Stories are intended to engage us emotionally, and a storyteller takes us back to the circumstances of an event so that we can re-experience the event with him. If he is able to re-create the circumstances, the message will be clear.

Take a peek at the following two versions of the same story. The story tells about a moment when the narrator conquers a personal fear.

Version A: *My boss is a powerful and outspoken man who doesn't like it when people disagree with him. He is known for quickly putting down any dissenting point of view. So yesterday, when I had to go into a meeting with him and challenge him on the latest marketing strategy he had put together for our department, I was terrified. But I knew I had to speak my truth. I took a deep breath before I went into the meeting, and when he asked me what I thought of the marketing plan I looked him straight in the eye and said: "Look, Jim, I don't think this is going to work." He paused for a moment, looked me right back in the eye and said: "Yeah, I know." And I realized that all of my fear had been for naught.*

Version B: *My boss is a powerful and outspoken man who doesn't like it when people disagree with him. He is known for quickly putting down any dissenting point of view. So yesterday, right before I had to go into a meeting with him and challenge him on the latest marketing strategy he had put together for our department, I broke out into a sweat. It soaked right through my undershirt and began to trickle down the sleeves of my brand-new yellow dress shirt. My chest got very tight, and I felt my heart pound hard and fast. I was sure everyone around me could hear it furiously pummeling inside of me. I felt more and more sweat trickling down my arms, and then my chest started to heave. Up and down, up and down. "Get a hold of yourself," a little voice said inside my head. I closed my eyes and took a long deep breath, then another.*

"Whatever happens, it will be OK," the little voice in my head said to me. So after one last breath I walked into the meeting room and shook Jim's hand. When he asked me what I thought of the marketing plan, I paused for a moment, looked him straight in the eye, and thought of what my little voice had said to me. I held Jim's gaze, then told him: "Look, Jim, I don't think this is going to work." He paused for a moment, looked me right back in the eye and said: "Yeah, I know." And I saw a little smile sweep across his face.

I hope the difference between the two versions of the story is clear. Both do a decent job of getting the basic information about an event across to the listener. Remember—the point of the story is to tell about a moment when the narrator conquers a personal fear. Version A, however, does not dare take the listener back into the experience of this fear. Instead, it efficiently covers the basic information and then ends with a final sentence that explains the lesson of the story. Version B takes the listener right into the moment of fear that the narrator experienced. It re-creates the physical sensations for the listener, and it walks the listener through the thoughts and sensations that propelled the narrator forward to face his boss. In the end, this version doesn't explain the lesson of the story— it trusts that the listener *understands* the lesson because of its detailed telling.

Chances are Version B will create a lot more empathy between the listener and the narrator. We feel like we really are with the narrator as he takes us back to his moment of fear. Because he takes us back into his experience, we likely will remember comparable moments in our lives in which we had similar thoughts and physical sensations. His detailed description becomes an invitation into our own psyche, our own memories, our own experience. By trusting the power of detail, he is able to create a common ground with the audience. The story, and the faith this narrator has in its detailed telling, allows listeners truly to settle in and relax with him. Chances are, as well, that they will be more receptive to whatever information follows the telling of the story.

The biggest misconception about telling a story in a business environment is that an audience doesn't have patience for a story. So what do we do? We tell it as quickly as possible. We "get it over with." That, of course, defeats the entire purpose of telling the story in the first place. Most stories are not told in enough detail. The only part that is best covered swiftly is any necessary background information that will help our audience "step into the story." If the background cannot be told quickly, it likely is not a story worth telling. Know the reason why you are telling the story. Know the point this story will help you to illustrate. And then, trust the story. Linger, languish, and take the audience back into the full experience of being there with you. Re-create the sensual, physical, environmental circumstances of the story. Paint a lively, vivid picture. Our imaginations will do the rest of the work!

PRACTICE EXERCISES

In the upcoming exercises, I urge you to play ruthlessly with ways of framing every single presentation you deliver. You will have the opportunity to hone your framing mindset and resources, develop a repertoire of personal stories that have meaning for you, and fine-tune your storytelling skills.

Exercise 1: Developing a Frame Mindset

Don't consider presenting a speech without selecting one or more compelling frames. Think of a speech that you have to present in the near future. Most likely, you already have a good idea about the core content you will communicate through this speech. In this practice exercise, you will investigate frames that will help clarify your key points and "add life" to your presentation. Here, once again, are key framing devices you may wish to consider as you prepare:

- A story
- A quote
- An analogy or metaphor

- A statistic
- A visual aid (such as a prop or cartoon)
- A quick demonstration

You may wish to consider the following selection criteria as you choose frames for your presentation:

- Will this frame help clarify a concept or idea in my presentation?
- Will this frame help to engage my audience?
- Will this frame help to "add life" to my content?
- Will this frame stimulate both me and my audience?

The last criterion is the one that tends to drive my final decision about using a frame. If a frame excites me, and if I believe that the frame will be exciting to my audience—wow, what a great opportunity for creating a charged and powerful connection in a presentation!

Before you bring in an audience, prepare a five-to-ten-minute presentation. I urge you to use this as an opportunity to practice a presentation you actually have to give in the near future. Chances are your final presentation will be longer than the chunk you practice here with your sample audience. That's OK. Make sure that you have integrated at least three framing devices into the segment you have prepared for this exercise. Now you're ready to go.

- Invite three friends or colleagues to be your sample audience. Let them know that your purpose for this exercise is the experimentation with frames that help focus and engage the listener.
- Present your speech. As you present, be mindful of how your audience responds to the frames that you have woven into your speech.
- When you have completed your mini-presentation, invite feedback from your audience members. Focus their feedback on the frames within your speech. Did they enjoy the frames? Did the frames help engage them? Did the frames stir their imagination and curiosity? Did they have an emotional response to your

frames? Is there anything you could have done to strengthen the impact of these frames? Given the content of your speech, are there any other frames that might have better supported the content?

- Take a moment to contemplate and integrate the feedback you have received. Think of what you will do differently as you present the same content a second time. If you received tips and pointers for a whole new frame, take a risk and experiment with it in your second presentation.
- Present your speech again. As you present, focus on strengthening and maximizing the use of your frames.
- During the feedback process, invite your audience members to compare the impact of your frames in this round to their impact the first time around. How well did the frames work this time? Did they engage your audience members in a more compelling manner? Did they better stimulate their hearts and minds? Is there anything else you might do to more effectively use these frames? Do they have suggestions for any other frames that might stir their imaginations and peak their curiosity?
- Complete this exercise by assessing your strengths in the skill you practiced, as well as any insights on how you would like to further develop your mastery of this skill.

Exercise 2: Creating a Story Bank

Here's an opportunity for you to begin collecting stories that may find their way into a presentation you give in the future. This is *your* homework, and will not require an audience. You can certainly do this homework as you prepare for a specific presentation, but I urge all speakers to simply get in the habit of gathering and knowing stories. This way, you will have a wonderful story at your fingertips, even if it isn't part of a prepared presentation. You will, in fact, start to become a storyteller. Furthermore, I hope that you will derive great pleasure from gathering these personal stories that distill meaningful incidents from your life.

The best stories tell about a moment in your life when something surprising happened. Something unexpected. Something that challenged your beliefs and values. Something that taught you a lesson. This can certainly be a "big" life-changing moment that redefined the course of your life. But more often than not, it will be the story of a little moment, a small gesture, a chance encounter, a fleeting exchange that provided you with a valuable insight.

Some stories may leap to mind right away. Others may require a bit of excavation on your part. It may help you to explore and discover stories by contemplating specific places or periods in your life. I, for example, might contemplate moments and stories from my life in the theater. Moments and stories from my travels to foreign countries. Moments and stories from my visits to all of my corporate clients. Moments and stories from coaching sessions with my clients. Moments and stories from the time when I first became a coach and trainer. The list goes on and on. But your choice of a specific context will help to focus your inquiry and guide you to a specific story.

So—enjoy this trip down memory lane. Find a quiet, private place and time for this reflection. For me, this would mean lying down on my bed in the afternoon. Also pick a specific time frame for this focused daydream—say half an hour or so. Then close your eyes and travel back over moments and incidents. I like to keep a notebook right next to my bed when I conduct such a memory exercise. Anytime a moment or story leaps to mind that somehow seems significant, I jot down a quick note on my notebook. Then I return to my luxurious, focused daydream.

When my half-hour exploration is over, I review my notes and ask myself a few simple questions: Is there a story in here that I might share in a public setting? Could I tell this story without a very elaborate setup or background information? What is the lesson or learning point of this story?

Thus you are well on your way to creating a collection of personal stories that resonate with you, have strong personal meaning, and could become key frames for a future public presentation. I urge you to keep track of these stories in a central location—you will be amazed at how quickly you will amass a wealth of anecdotes.

Sometimes a client will tell me that she doesn't have a lot of personal stories to tell. "I simply haven't had a very interesting life!" I trust that it is clear to you, my reader, that I do not accept such statements. Most likely, this client has the mistaken impression that the stories need to tell of exotic or outlandish experiences. They don't. It is also likely that this client has not spent enough time reflecting on the meaning or lessons of the simple moments in her life. I immediately send her back to unearth at least three stories that she has never told in public before—stories that may contain a universal lesson or moral. Invariably, the very client who protested returns with stories that completely woo me, move me, and delight me!

I do, however, encourage you to add two other categories to the story bank you are creating. I have very successfully used stories that I read in a book or magazine, or stories that were told to me by a friend or colleague. I always acknowledge the source of a story and do not pretend that I am recounting a firsthand experience—but then I tell this appropriated story as vividly as if I had actually been there. Even if it is not a personal experience, I still want to take my audience fully back into the experience of this story. In the end, it will not matter that it is an appropriated story; if told with clarity and urgency, the lesson will still be the same.

Besides keeping track of such secondhand stories, I encourage you to also keep a file of quotes. Quotes are terrific speaker aides because they tend to be succinct. They almost always elicit a chuckle or a little "aha" moment of recognition from an audience. A quote is not really a story—but a good quote causes the listener to reflect on a personal story that relates to the message or nugget of wisdom within the quote. The quote thus acts as a personal-story catalyst for the listener. It is a spare and efficient way to generate resonance with a large group of people!

Exercise 3: Telling the Story

This is the beauty of the homework you have completed in the preceding practice exercise: Suddenly, you have lots and lots of stories to tell! So let's go ahead and practice telling some of those stories.

Here's a question I'm often asked when it is storytelling time: Should we write stories down and memorize them, word by word? Or is it better to simply know the key incidents and trust the spontaneous telling of a story "in the moment"? There is no right approach or method to story preparation. If you have not previously told a lot of stories to an audience, writing the story down and memorizing it may give you both confidence and peace of mind. If you do not have a lot of experience in re-creating the details of an event for an audience, writing it down will help you to get clear on just how detailed you need to be in the telling of an event. If you fear getting nervous in front of an audience, learning and memorizing a story beforehand is likely a wise cautionary strategy. I discourage you strongly, however, from reading the story to an audience. It is the speaker's job to relive and re-create the story as she tells it. If she finds herself deviating from the prepared text, so be it!

And here's a second question I frequently hear about the delivery style of a story: Should I "act out" the story as I'm telling it? How far should I go with using my body movements, gestures, and vocal inflections to illustrate what happens in the story? Once again, there is no one right approach or answer. Some speakers love to go all out and unleash their "inner ham" when it is time to tell a story. Fine. Their audiences will certainly appreciate the entertainment that is offered by such an illustrative approach. If taken too far, however, this speaker runs the danger of overshadowing the content and the message of the story with her performance bravado. It is almost like witnessing the Broadway version of the story—flashy, but with little or no space left for the listener to imagine what isn't said, or fill in the quieter moments with a personal association.

So, don't fear a simpler or more straightforward telling of your story. Just remember the three key storytelling guidelines from earlier in this chapter, and you will be fine: Know the point of the story and why you're telling it. Keep the setup and introduction short and sweet. Then take us back to the circumstances of your story so we can relive it all with you!

Now that you have prepared your story, bring in your audience of two or three friends or colleagues for a little round of storytelling. Here are some pointers for getting the most out of this storytelling practice:

- Make sure your audience knows that you are here to practice the delivery of a story.
- Tell the story. As you tell it, notice the reactions of your audience to the details of the story. You can tell at once what sort of impact you are having on your audience members—are they moved, amused, excited, entertained? Confused, dumbfounded?
- When you're done, tell your audience first what you believe you did well, then what you might do differently in a second telling. Encourage feedback from your audience members. Ask them to address the three focal areas of your storytelling approach: Did they have enough background information to be able to step into the story? Was the background presented in a succinct and efficient manner? Was the lesson or main point of the story clear? Did you succeed in re-creating the particular circumstances and experience of the story for them? What emotional impact did your story have for them? Do they have any tips for you that might enhance your delivery of this story for them?
- Take a moment to contemplate the feedback you received. Then tell the story again, with an eye to integrating both your own feedback and the insights you received from your audience.
- Repeat a similar feedback process, beginning with a quick self-assessment and then encouraging specific feedback from your audience. Be sure to compare the two tellings of the same story. Were there things you said and did in the second telling that made it more effective than the first? Were there things that made the first telling more effective than the second?

- Complete this exercise by reflecting on your strengths as a story-teller, as well as noting any insights on how you may further develop your mastery of this skill. If your audience is game, repeat the process using another story. It is quite possible that your audience will have a very different reaction to your story-telling skills with a brand-new story. If you decide to initiate this new practice round, make sure that here, again, there is time for sufficient feedback and a "take-two" opportunity to integrate any of the insights you may have received!

CHAPTER 8

Embracing Humor

In a seminar on the topic of humor in public speaking, I asked participants to think of their favorite comic. Over half of this group immediately mentioned Robin Williams. When I probed a little further to get a sense of what my participants so enjoyed about Robin Williams, these were some of the qualities mentioned: Robin Williams was *spontaneous, irreverent, improvisational, smart,* and *topical.*

Wouldn't we enjoy some of those same qualities in any public speaker? Now, our business presentations will likely not be as over the top as a Robin Williams nightclub appearance. But let us contemplate the antonyms of the adjective list my seminar participants generated: totally *scripted, serious, by-the-book, dumb,* and *out-of-date.* That sounds like a recipe for a truly numbing presentation, doesn't it?

I have a hunch this last list is one reason why corporations are spending tens of thousands of dollars on humor consultants to help coach their speakers to have a "light touch." Chances are they're not trying to turn every CEO or senior manager into a stand-up comic. But they understand that an audience will only tune into statistics and productivity reports and profit-margin analyses for so long. Humor engages an audience. Humor relaxes an audience. Humor establishes common ground—it humanizes the thematic content and the formality of the situation. And laughter feels good—it helps release tension and stress from the body.

Yet, the idea of using humor in a "serious" business presentation still makes many presenters mighty uncomfortable. Here are some of the rationales I most frequently hear:

Objection #1: My Content Is Truly Dry and Boring

That, of course, is the prime reason for adding a light touch to the presentation. If the content is dry, let us not go ahead and emphasize the dryness. I trust that the dryness factor will be blazingly evident and speak for itself. Let us season the speech with a light touch, instead, to make it more palatable, add a bit of sizzle, bring out hidden flavors, and, above all, help with the digestive process.

Objection #2: If I Use Too Much Humor, It Will Take Away from My Credibility as a Presenter. I Will Not Be Viewed as Serious

When I hear this line of reasoning, I think of a seminar I facilitated with a group of instructional designers at NASA. Before I flew down to Huntsville, Alabama, to work with these folks, I received a phone call from a colleague who had just worked with the same team: "This is the smartest and most overeducated group of people I have ever worked with," she said to me. "When you get there, do not try any fluff stuff. No puzzles, no trivia, no funny stories. Just stick to the content."

Well, that was the wrong thing to say to me. One of my character flaws is that the moment you tell me I should not do something, I get this overwhelming urge to do it. And my colleague was right—this was a super-duper smart group. These individuals created the very elaborate training programs that prepare U.S. astronauts to head into outer space. But I noticed something else right away: the seminar I was facilitating included a manual that came with a slew of puzzles, trivia questions, and humorous diversions. Light stuff. None of it related in any way to the very serious content of the seminar—Instructional Design. Within minutes, my NASA design team had spotted these diversions and was compulsively trying to solve the puzzle sheets. The message was clear. My participants were not avoiding the "light" diversions. On the contrary, my super-duper over-educated audience clearly craved the light stuff. My instincts told me that their highly taxed brains might need even more light diversions than my average audience; instead of removing the light touches, I added more!

Objection #3: I'm Simply Not Funny

I have a hunch that this belief lies at the core of any hesitation about using humor. More importantly, I hear the speaker's fear of having to be and do something that he is not. Something that's not natural for him. And I agree—there is almost nothing as painful for me as watching a speaker try to be funny, when he's not. He's probably not funny because he's trying to be funny in a way that would work for another presenter but not for him. He is forcing a humor style that is not authentic for him. And he doesn't understand that there are many other ways to have a light touch.

Can we learn to be funny? Well, I believe we can understand the different ways in which humor is expressed, and I believe we can understand our personal affinities for humor. In the exercise portion of this chapter, you will have the opportunity to look at different humor styles to help you clarify your "humor voice." If exploring your humor voice makes you entirely uncomfortable, remember that there are many ways in which humor can be imported. A cartoon projected on a slide will often do the trick for you. A humorous quote you find and appropriate will speak volumes. A familiar and pertinent movie clip will have your audience in stitches. If you have one or several participants in your audience who reveal a light touch, call on them often. They will likely appreciate the attention, and they will act as your very own unofficial warm-up act.

HUMOR IN ACTION

If you are a speaker with a strongly developed funny bone and a loose lip, here's a cautionary tale. I will never forget a business seminar that I conducted in New York for a group of thirty corporate trainers. They had come together from a wide variety of business backgrounds to sharpen their presentation skills. Two of the trainers, as it turned out, moonlighted in the evenings as stand-up comics in the New York City club scene. We laughed with great joy during those three seminar days. Karen was a sales trainer for a renowned German automobile maker, and Phil facilitated courses about medical product information for a health care provider. Both Karen and Phil faced a formidable challenge: How would they put their wildly humorous and inventive instincts in the service of the information their employers had asked them to impart? At what point did they transgress that invisible line where their funny bone actually obscured the message of the presentation?

I found out a year later, when I crossed paths again with Karen: she had successfully fused her comic style with the demands of being a high-end sales trainer, and had, in fact, become one of the most popular sales trainers for this automobile maker. Phil, on the other hand, had left the training field altogether. He had wisely realized that his comic sensibility seemed to be forever at odds with the demands of the training information he had to deliver. His true arena was the comedy club scene in Los Angeles, where he went to seek fame and fortune.

If you have any lingering doubts about the benefit of choosing a light approach, I ask you to contemplate the delivery style of Dr. Jody Spiro. Well into my career as a speaking coach, I decided to go back to graduate school. Part of the jolt of being back in school was the harsh reality of experiencing my graduate school instructors. Many spoke in a monotonous and deadly dull manner, as if being a highly schooled subject-matter expert alone was sufficient effort to spark interest in their captive audience.

Enter Dr. Spiro.

Just as I was giving up on the idea that I might encounter a first-rate presenter at New York University, I enrolled in

Dr. Spiro's course on the nature of International Nongovernmental Organizations. Now, that is not an inherently sexy or exciting topic. Worse yet, the course was offered Thursday evenings from 8:10 to 9:50. By any university standard, that's the graveyard shift. Most of Dr. Spiro's students were working professionals who toiled in underresourced nongovernmental office jobs during the week. By Thursday evening, Dr. Spiro faced a sea of tired bodies and minds as she attempted to interest her students in the finer aspects of the world of international nongovernmental organizations.

This was by far the best class I took in graduate school.

How did Dr. Spiro manage to engage her weary brood? Yes, you guessed it—Dr. Spiro used a light approach to a not inherently light topic. More importantly, she keenly understood her own comic style. Dr. Spiro is a consummate storyteller, and there was no class in which she did not tell several well-prepared comic tales that highlighted a key teaching point. She always took her time with a story, relishing details, adding colorful flourishes, carefully building to the punchline. Dr. Spiro quite shamelessly milked every story for the comic potential within. She also knew that at such a late class time, students needed a few minutes to mentally and emotionally shift gears and settle into the classroom learning environment. Thus, the first ten minutes of each class were filled with funny topical banter initiated by Dr. Spiro—about politics, weather, an incident in the preceding week's class, or an anecdote from her always-interesting non-university life. Dr. Spiro's command of her comic style, and her commitment to calling upon it without fail, turned every class into a feast of engaged learning.

Storytelling and light banter may not be a part of your own humor style. But we have already mentioned some of the other ways in which we bring levity to our delivery. In the upcoming exercise, you will have the opportunity to examine those things that you find humorous—and then I urge you to contemplate how your preferences may become part of your personal speaking style.

PRACTICE EXERCISE

Here's a chance to take a closer look at some of the different humor presentation styles used by comics or comedic actors. We don't want to ape or mimic their styles when we present, but chances are, you will have more affinity with some styles than with others. So this is your opportunity to conduct a quick humor-style study. Be aware of the different styles employed by folks that are funny. Notice what styles appeal to you. Then you will be able to make an educated choice about how your preferred styles match your own comfort zone. There will be opportunities to study some of the comics you like, and there may be ways in which some of their techniques will actually work for you when it is your turn to speak.

Identify Your Humor Presentation Style

For each of the seven following categories, check all of the statements that apply to you:

Topical Humor
❏ Get humor from the news, radio, or newspaper.
❏ Make jokes about current events.
❏ Make light of celebrities, politicians.
❏ Poke fun at the latest trends.
❏ See humor in the most mundane things.

Character Humor
❏ Like to tell stories and jokes in character.
❏ Like to wear costumes.
❏ Like to combine different gestures and facial expressions for certain characters.
❏ Like to use different voices and accents when telling stories.
❏ Use an alter ego to show another point of view.

Physical Humor

- ❑ Incorporate slapstick comedy.
- ❑ Use self-deprecating humor.
- ❑ Set up pratfalls.
- ❑ Use lots of body gestures and facial expressions.
- ❑ Mime actions when telling a story.

Impression Humor

- ❑ Assume different characters when telling stories.
- ❑ Like to imitate people.
- ❑ Like to create your own characters.
- ❑ Good at accents.
- ❑ Pick up people's idiosyncrasies easily.

Improvisational Humor

- ❑ Play off other people's reactions.
- ❑ Use ad-libs often.
- ❑ Like to use unrehearsed, unscripted jokes.
- ❑ Use others' suggestions to create stories and jokes.
- ❑ Make up songs off the top of your head.

Prop Humor

- ❑ Like to wear costumes.
- ❑ Use noisemakers.
- ❑ Play with toys and props.
- ❑ Like to do magic tricks.
- ❑ Use visual aids.

Observational Humor

- ❑ Observe people or situations to get funny material.
- ❑ Make light of people or situations.
- ❑ Use jokes based on true situations.

❏ Comment on family, work relationships, and friends.
❏ Get material from life experiences.

Scoring

Total your responses in each category to identify your preferred humor presentation styles.

Topical Humor Total: _____ Dennis Miller, Jay Leno, David Letterman, Joy Behar, Chris Rock
Character Humor Total: _____ Whoopi Goldberg, Tim Allen, Margaret Cho, Billy Crystal, Steven Wright
Physical Humor Total: _____ Jim Carrey, Martin Short, John Cleese, Rowan Atkinson, Leslie Nielsen
Impression Humor Total: _____ Dana Carvey, Rich Little, Mike Myers
Improvisational Humor Total: _____ Robin Williams, Wayne Brady, Don Rickles, Steve Harvey
Prop Humor Total: _____ Carrot Top, Rip Taylor, Gallagher
Observational Humor Total: _____ Eddie Murphy, Ellen DeGeneres, Jerry Seinfeld, Bill Cosby, Rosie O'Donnell

Tips

- Choose a comic that uses the same presentation as you, or a style you especially enjoy.
- Watch videos and TV shows that headline the comic you have chosen.
- Incorporate the strategies and techniques the comic uses into your own presentations.
- Read books by these comedians to get a feel for their style of comedy.

("Humor Presentation Style" exercise courtesy of Langevin Learning Services.)

CHAPTER 9

Inviting Dialogue

When I reach this chapter, I hesitate. All of my quick and not-so-hidden assumptions suddenly come into play. Do we really have to talk about the importance of *questioning* and *listening*, I ask myself? Don't we all know this stuff?

The answer, I believe, is no. Or, to be more precise, even if we do know, the moment we speak in public it is oh-so-easy to forget.

Even the most enlightened speaker, given a podium and a microphone, will don the mantle of the expert and talk on and on without relying on the simple tools that we will visit in this chapter. It's as if she suddenly had amnesia. The expert role, the lure of the stage, the power of the podium—they are that intoxicating. An inner switch, the switch that says "I'm the expert, and folks are here to hear my expertise," gets turned on the moment she stands up to speak. More often than not, audience members are "captives," especially when the speaker has institutional clout. They will listen because of the institutional role the speaker plays. They will not necessarily be attentive because she inhabits that role. They may be silent and polite, but they will not automatically engage.

Even if the speaker is the world's most renowned expert on a particular topic or niche, it is her job to relate this expertise to the demands, concerns, and questions of this particular audience. Unless she is truly a brilliant mind reader, it behooves her to ask some questions of her audience, encourage their questions, listen closely, and offer clarifying answers. If she doesn't, she runs the risk of doing what I owned up to doing at the beginning of this chapter: operating under a bunch of assumptions.

Now, we have all heard the speaker who likes to begin a speech by announcing "the lay of the land" for the presentation: "I will talk for about forty-five minutes or so, and then we'll have some time for questions and answers afterward." If this speaker is adept at managing his speaking time, this usually means there will be maybe ten minutes at best toward the end of the presentation for the audience to respond. If the speaker has gotten carried away with his presentation, this time is usually absorbed into the presentation and, oops, suddenly there is no time for any dialogue at all!

We have also likely been in the presence of the speaker who, after a lengthy presentation, decides to open the floor up for questions. Frequently, there is a long, embarrassed silence in the hall. Audience members seem to shy away from actually asking a question. Those who are courageous enough to raise a question sound tepid as they stand up to speak. There is a general sense of fizzled energy and lost focus as a presentation falls apart in this final question-and-answer session. Instead of ending with a grand finale, the presentation goes out with a whimper. Worse yet, the main message or meaning of the speech is likely lost or forgotten, as the entire event fades into oblivion.

FLIPPING THE PARADIGM

Such speaking situations are shouting for a paradigm adjustment, from a monologue to a dialogue approach. Most importantly, a dialogue approach needs to be established early on in a presentation. Don't be surprised if after talking for forty-five minutes, nobody in the audience has a question. By now, the audience has been beaten into silent submission. It has been forced into the role of the quiet, passive receiver, a role that is uncomfortable for many adults who long to be heard. A seasoned speaker knows that she needs to create a response habit early in the presentation, preferably within the first five to ten minutes. Forty-five minutes into a presentation is simply too late. By then, the audience members are plotting their escape from the auditorium. They will do everything possible not to extend this experience. They'll even get upset with those fellow attendees who dare ask questions this late in the game!

Here's the second part of the paradigm shift. The traditional question-and-answer session generally involves a few questions from the audience that are, in turn, graciously answered by the speaker. This keeps the speaker squarely in the authority role. Well, what about asking a probing question of the audience? What about enticing the audience, with the help of a question, to analyze, synthesize, or clarify a key statement you just made? What about inviting the audience to tell you how it will apply the principles that you have outlined in your speech, back in "the real world?" Your questions to the audience send a very different message about how you view this relationship! They let your audience members know that there is real value there for them to engage—you are actually curious about their thoughts, and you will occasionally want to hear what they have to say.

I acknowledge that the application of what I just outlined is not as simple as it may sound. The consistent integration of questioning and listening is truly a lifelong learning process. The barriers to practicing this approach in a public speaking environment can be enormous. Often, you have to contend with all sorts of external distractions while you speak. Bad acoustics. Doors that bang. Cell phones that ring. Participants who arrive late or slip out midstream. The larger the audience, the tougher it can be to initiate a dialogue relationship with the entire group. In a hall with an audience of several hundred, many of the participants simply seem too far away from you. And, in fact, they truly are! Conversely, you also seem very far away to them. This large audience needs the dialogue approach the most—the physical circumstances of such an auditorium conspire with brutal force against creating a speaker-audience connection. They offer your listener every incentive to quickly disengage from you!

External distractions will be compounded by our own inner triggers and distractions. We may not feel our best on a particular day.

We may not be entirely comfortable with a particular audience. We may have a "personal beef" with one or several of our audience members. Engaging in a dialogue process may feel like the absolutely last thing we wish to undertake; it can seem so much easier to just "do it all on our own." Moreover, almost every audience already has a complex relationship with an expert speaker. As my colleague Dawn Denvir so succinctly put it to me: "Audiences want us to be the expert, and they resent us for being the expert." Harsh as that may sound, I believe there is a fundamental kernel of truth in this observation. So, not only do we deal with all of the inner and outer distractions, we're also constantly navigating this complex and entirely subterranean dynamic between the speaker and the audience!

I don't profess to have quick or tidy answers to the dilemmas I just raised. I do know, however, that a consistent application of a dialogue approach is the one surefire way of generating and sustaining a climate of engagement and respect. I do not relish the alternative—presenting in an environment of disengagement and the absence of such respect. When I speak, I am committed to doing everything within my power to help engage my audience. So, here are some pointers on how you can best navigate the dialogue process:

Asking Questions
- Build dialogue early in your speech by asking questions that folks can readily answer.
- Choose questions that can generate both short and long answers.
- Present a question as a quick mini-brainstorm: "Let's see if we can come up with at least five different ideas!"
- Make sure that everyone can hear your question, and that everyone can hear the response by an audience member. Don't assume. Check with your audience.
- State the question. Pause and wait for an answer. The willingness to wait and pause is one of the marks of a commanding speaker. Restate the question if you have not received a response after this initial pause.

- In a large auditorium, ask questions that require participants to respond in agreement or disagreement by raising their hand, standing up, waving, or applauding. These are quick ways of taking the pulse of a large group. Such group responses invite your audience to stay engaged—and they have a simple, energizing aerobic side benefit!
- Avoid token questions that are merely an excuse to get you back to your prepared script. The audience will sense this immediately. Your rhetorical question will be a turnoff. The moment you ask a question, you need to fully work with the answer you receive.
- If there is an opportunity for a follow-up question, and you have time for the follow-up—go for it! It lets your audience members know that you value their participation, that you value the first question enough to want to follow up, and that you really heard and understand what they said!

Answering Questions

- Validate a great question that has been posed! Your validation sends a powerfully positive message to your entire audience, not just to the individual who raised the question.
- Give eye contact to the person who asked the question. Respond to this individual, but then swing out and share your answer with the entire group.
- Try to be brief and to the point with your answer. A long and rambling response will discourage other participants from asking questions!
- The most successful answer is factual and offers a specific benefit to the person who raised the question.
- Respond to questions and comments from every part of your audience, not just the few individuals who may wish to monopolize the dialogue.
- Create thematic connections for your audience with your response. Use your answers as an opportunity to elaborate, clarify, or underscore points you made earlier in your presentation.

- Refrain from elaborately answering questions that you will address later in your presentation anyway!
- If you are presented with a question that uses hostile or negative language, refrain from repeating that negative language in your response. Choose neutral language, instead.

Dialogue Don'ts

- Do not judge the question you receive.
- Watch for body language that may reveal your judgment of the question.
- Listen to the full question. Don't interrupt or jump to conclusions.
- Do not send a follow-up question to a participant that uses hostile language. Answer succinctly and move on!
- Do not get caught in a ping-pong exchange with one questioner. Keep inviting other participants into the dialogue.
- Resist the temptation to "be right" or have the final word; be willing to disagree with a participant and move on!
- Don't bluff! Don't be afraid of admitting that "I don't have this information right now," or that "I can't answer this question at this time."
- Do not ignore a question that is raised. Reframing the question as you respond is a great way of shifting gears—ignoring the question, however, is not!

REFRAMING THE QUESTION

Not only do we create frames that help us clarify and shape the content we present, the moment we engage in a dialogue process we constantly reframe questions or comments we receive from an audience. I don't suggest that we dodge or altogether ignore a question when we reframe. We have all listened to unskilled politicians who never seem to answer a single question they are asked. Sadly, they have been coached to do this. Listening to a conversation between an ill-coached politician and a reporter often sounds like two cars speeding down a highway, traveling in parallel lanes. Sometimes one car passes the other; sometimes the other passes the first. The drivers might glance at each other, exchange a quick smile. But they never stop, never open the window, never connect.

A good reframe is a thoughtful response to an audience comment. It challenges both the speaker and the audience to look at a point, topic, or idea from a different perspective. It offers a crystallizing point of view. It may redirect a question or comment by offering a not-yet-contemplated solution or benefit. Reframing is frequently used to steer an audience away from a perspective or point of view that the speaker does not wish to address, but that is not its primary function. A powerful reframing comment opens new perspectives, deepens understanding, and offers an expanding view of a topic. And yes— it can certainly be a protective move to deflect from a content area we don't wish to examine just then!

Here are some tips on how you can successfully reframe comments and questions in the dialogue process:

- First and foremost, remember that not every audience question or comment needs to be reframed. Decide how much controversy or possible disagreement you can live with. Allowing for dissent and disagreement is one of the marks of an exceptional leader!
- If someone expresses doubt about a point you made—acknowledge that you have also had doubt. If someone announces that a proposal is silly—tell her that you, too, thought it was silly at first. By agreeing with the speaker, you are deflating any of the potentially adversarial thunder. Then complete your response with a simple benefit statement. You will have just executed a very elegant and subtle reframe!
- The best reframing answer listens to a statement and picks out the underlying issue. If you receive a barrage of comments from a participant, listen to what might be lurking behind this barrage. Here are some classic issues that frequently arise in a business presentation: unrealistic timing or timeline of a project; prohibitive cost; lack of feasibility; scarcity of resources; or priority of

project. And here are the emotions that usually simmer below the surface: frustration, anger, exhaustion, or lingering burnout. Name the issue and/or the emotion, and then offer a specific solution, strategy, or benefit.

- If you're not sure you properly understood a question or comment, do a little reality check. "Did I hear this correctly? Did I interpret this correctly? Did I get this right?" This inquiry not only shows your concern for the comment from the audience— it also buys you time to come up with the best possible reframe you can dream up in the moment!

REFRAMING WITH AWARENESS

Here is a sample question that might be asked of a politician: *Do you think you have any chance at all of winning this election?* I offer you four different responses, and a quick analysis of the implications of each reframe:

1. *Answer*: Look, not only do I want to win this election, I believe I will win all of the other upcoming elections until I receive the nomination!
   - *Analysis of answer*: It dodges the "chance part" of the question but builds on the winning part. It opens the winning frame by focusing not only on this one election but on a whole slew of elections. It takes the smaller, short-term focus of the question and widens it!
2. *Answer*: I think I'm talking about the issues that matter to audiences most.
   - *Analysis of answer*: This is a more implicit response than answer # 1. It implies that because I talk about what matters to voters, I will have a good chance of winning. It will likely be perceived as an avoidance of the question!
3. *Answer*: Look, I know a lot of you believe I don't have a chance of winning, but take a look at some other candidates throughout history who came from behind. Who would have thought

early on that Bill Clinton would be the Democratic nominee and eventual president?

- *Analysis of Answer*: It shows that the speaker is not afraid of answering a tough question. And it opens up the frame by shifting from a "here-and-now" outlook to a more rosy and impersonal historic perspective.

4. *Answer*: Every time I have run for office I have been the underdog, and I have always come from behind and beat the establishment candidate!

- *Analysis of Answer*: It offers a personal historic perspective of "always winning," and it widens the frame by implicitly contrasting the speaker's outsider role with the opponent's insider status.

The beauty of the dialogue approach is that it will, when applied and practiced with consistency, steer the speaker away from the "canned presentation." It forces every speaker to stay present in the moment. It keeps every presentation alive, because it invites the element of variability and surprise. In the best sense of the word, it will keep the speaker on her toes. Moreover, the skill and finesse with which she encourages questions and then responds will always enhance her standing with her audience. A dialogue approach is a classic win-win strategy for any public speaker!

PRACTICE EXERCISE

To practice the dialogue approach, invite a sample audience of two or three friends or colleagues. Prepare to speak on a topic of your choice for five to ten minutes. More importantly, prepare at least three questions you will put to your audience within the first five minutes. Let your audience members know that, for the purpose of this exercise, they need to be willing to raise questions throughout, contribute comments, and actively engage with you. Make sure your friends understand that this is not a preparation for handling a resistant audience—we'll work on that a little later. No, their job is simply to ask questions, request clarification, offer their opinions, which may or may not be in agreement with the content of your presentation. Their active involvement and participation will be a key success factor in this practice exercise!

Here are some additional tips for your dialogue practice exercise:

- Present your speech. Make sure someone keeps track of time, and stop when ten minutes are up. When we engage in dialogue, we frequently lose all sense of time!
- Focus on asking your questions early on, and investigate the different ways in which you can answer, follow-up, and reframe during your presentation. This will be more important than diligently "sticking to the script!"
- When your first ten minutes are up, offer your own feedback first. How well did you handle the responses to the questions you had planned? How did you handle the questions and comments your audience threw at you? Did you take advantage of follow-up opportunities? Did you have a chance to reframe audience comments and observations?
- Elicit feedback from your audience members. Did they feel engaged by your questions? Were they satisfied with the way in which you handled their comments and responses? Was your dialogue approach successful in keeping them engaged with your presentation? Are there any additional things you could have said that would have deepened their involvement?
- Take a moment to reflect on the feedback you received. Then present the same speech again. Try to integrate the feedback you received, but remember that the moment we practice a dialogue approach, no presentation will ever be the same again! Above all, listen closely to the comments and reactions from your audience members, and respond in a way that will help deepen their involvement.

- After ten minutes, stop and repeat the feedback process from the first round. Offer your own feedback first and then elicit feedback from your audience. Note your successes in applying the comments you received after your first presentation. Note, as well, how you adapted to new questions, different observations, and other challenges that may have come up in this second presentation.

- Complete this exercise by reflecting on your strength in asking questions, inviting questions, offering answers, and reframing audience comments. Note any insights on how you wish to further develop your mastery of these skills!

CHAPTER 10

Transforming Resistance

This—I am quite certain—is the single biggest fear factor for anyone who has to speak in public: What if "they" don't want to play with me? I've invited a whole group of folks to my party, and not a single one of them wants to do the dance. Not only do they not want to dance, they snicker and sneer at my meticulously prepared dance routine. They sneer in silence. Or they heckle me out loud. They just don't like any of my steps. Because they don't like my steps, I become unsettled, and the dance steps I have so meticulously rehearsed suddenly don't execute as beautifully as they normally do. . . .

You see where this path is leading us: all of my carefully orchestrated preparations can readily unravel in the face of a resistant audience. (We'll spend a whole chapter in part III looking at our relationship to fear.) The moment I encounter resistance, I no longer have the luxury of simply executing a beautifully planned presentation. The moment the audience is not playing with me, the dance has to become a new dance.

These are my two options: I can try to shift the resistance, or I can name it.

There simply is no other way. The strategy some speakers opt for—let me pretend that everything is fine, and let me deliver my speech as planned—never works. All the willpower in the world cannot bury or banish the seething hostility in the room. Barging ahead on the part of the speaker in the face of resistance is actually a profound act of aggression. It's the "let me thumb my nose at the audience" approach. My hostility will invariably breed more audience hostility. This, in turn, will breed more hostility and resentment within me. My audience will sense this resentment and . . .

You see, once again, where the road is leading us.

Avoidance is a conflict-handling mechanism that many people use quite consistently in their professional and personal lives. A well-honed avoidance approach may, indeed, serve us in the occasional individual conflict situation. I don't believe it ever works for anyone as the primary, consistent strategy for handling conflict. It certainly is entirely ineffective when dealing with a group. Group hostility breeds on itself and quickly boomerangs into stratospheric proportions. My well-honed avoidance approach will desert me the moment I come face to face with a group. The collective energy of a group is simply too potent.

No—I can either find ways of shifting an audience's resistance, or I can address the resistance directly. Light resistance, or small pockets of resistance from a portion of the audience, may be shiftable. Please note that I use the word "may." Anyone who claims that there are surefire ways of addressing audience hostility or resistance is lying through his teeth or is delusional about his powers of persuasion. All we ever have available to us is a reserve of tools and techniques, and our instincts. They may do the job, or they may not. No audience is ever exactly like the next, and what works with one may fall entirely flat with another. All I know for sure is this: In the face of resistance, I need to find alternate ways of engaging or re-engaging my audience.

ACTS OF RE-ENGAGEMENT

What are some subtle ways of shifting resistance or re-engaging the audience? Quite simply, every single tool we have explored so far in part II is also a terrific way of shifting resistance, even though this may not necessarily be its primary function:

- A light quip, a self-deprecating comment, an off-the-cuff humorous observation—these can all be simple ways of showing audience members that they need not fear you (which may be one of the reasons you are receiving resistance), and that you are willing to have a good time with them. Mild resistance will often melt in the face of a lighthearted approach. The light touch can be the quickest way of defusing lingering anxiety in the audience.
- If there is an uncomfortable silence in the room, ask a safe, open-ended question that anyone can answer. Even a rude audience will find it tough not to answer an "easy question."
- If you don't receive a quick response, try to ride out the moment. Let the silence become a little uncomfortable. Chances are your audience will be a lot more uncomfortable with this silence than you are. Someone will likely jump in to "rescue" the moment. She will understand that by hanging out with this silence, you mean business. That, in fact, was the cue she needed to jump in and engage.
- If necessary, give a clear verbal cue to your audience that you are willing to wait out a moment of silence: "This question is important enough that I won't move on until we have entertained some of your answers." This verbal cue, of course, is delivered in the nicest possible manner, not as a threat!
- If necessary, ask participants to briefly turn to someone next to them and take thirty seconds to quickly discuss your question. This is especially effective if you have a small audience of no more than thirty or forty participants. Let participants know that afterward you will call on some of them to share their responses with the entire group. This sends a friendly but firm message to your audience that "tuning out" is not an option, and that you will, indeed, persist.
- Put a different frame around your topic. Sometimes audiences do not respond or shut down because we present material in a manner that is too abstract, not relevant to them, or because we

have not made the relevance apparent. Tighten the frame. Make the content more specific. Relate it to the needs of this audience.

- Play devil's advocate if you need to. If, for example, you are introducing a new company policy to your audience, ask a question that may get a rise out of this audience: "So why do you think this new policy was instituted?" "Why should you care about this new policy?" "Why should we bother with yet another new policy?" Most likely, someone in your audience will have something to say in response to these questions. Suddenly, you have created a dialogue. All you need now is a sincere willingness to engage with whatever responses are hurled your way.

- Try to move physically closer to your audience. Walk into your audience if you can. Sit among your audience members for a moment if that is possible. Such a physical move will probably startle and surprise them, but you will get their attention. You are violating the role the audience has put you in—that of the remote, distant speaker it is not interested in. It is always tougher to resist someone who is in close physical proximity. Your willingness to get close to the audience and abandon the safe "speaker distance" also sends another strong nonverbal message: I won't give up so easily. I will do whatever I can to draw you in. So please don't think you can just settle back and disengage, because I will persist and "make my moves."

THE VERBAL ATTACK

There are times when an audience member may resist by verbally attacking the speaker or challenging the speaker on every point he makes. Invariably, these acts of aggression are power plays, in which an audience member feels moved to challenge a speaker's authority. If this happens every time you speak, take a look at any signals you may be sending out that could provoke an audience member to want to challenge you. If it only happens once in awhile, however, such audience attacks have likely nothing to do with you whatsoever. You're simply in the presence of an audience member who always does this when he is faced with a speaker. That's his patterned behavior—his "shtick"—every time he sits in an audience.

I stress this to make sure you do not take his challenges or attacks personally. There are classic roles that some folks inhabit the moment they're in a group. They "play" the blocker, the dominator, the aggressor, the joker, the cynic, the attention seeker. Know, as well, that this individual's verbal taunting rarely has anything to do with the content of your speech, even though that is usually what this audience member purports to challenge. No, repeated interruptions, especially if they are delivered in a confrontational tone, are a fight for control and dominance.

Take the example of Nazma Muhammad-Rosado, a training manager with Pfizer Pharmaceuticals. In a recent conversation, Nazma, an American of Trinidadian descent, described just one such incident to me. She told of a moment that occurred a few months after the incidents of 9/11. A participant in a training seminar asked her, in front of the entire group of seminar participants: "So what would you do if terrorists flew their plane into your building?" Nazma, with her Arab name, understood this question, and the needling way in which it was delivered, as a deliberate anti-Arab taunt. "In the moment," Nazma explained, "I just answered it as if it were a serious question." The guy persisted and said, 'What I'm getting at is, would you act like an American or a damned terrorist too?' I continued to reply as if he were asking a question of utmost importance. I feel like I finally wore him down, simply because I continued to answer him, until he had nothing left to say and I had taken the wind out of his sails."

Nazma had rightfully understood that this participant was engaging in a power play. He was trying to rattle her nerves and provoke an annoyed or angered reaction. That, of course, is exactly how Nazma felt inside, but she won this little power struggle by not allowing the client to succeed. Nazma successfully rode out this wave of resistance and didn't fall for the bait. When she told me this story, I thought of a Southern saying that I learned when I first came to the United States: "Kill them with kindness."

That, indeed, is what Nazma did. Was her approach the only or the best way of handling this situation? "If he had caught me on a different day, in a different mood," Nazma explained, "I would have likely asked him to leave the training at once." That certainly would have been an equally valid way of addressing this situation. Nazma's willingness to ride out this wave of resistance, however, showed her true mastery of this situation. Several participants, she told me, complimented her afterward on how she had handled her confrontational participant. Her calm approach had clearly earned her added respect from the rest of her audience. A situation that might have unraveled an entire presentation actually enhanced Nazma's stature with this group. What a wonderful opportunity!

NAMING THE RESISTANCE

Individual pockets of resistance are one matter—deep-seated resistance by the majority of the audience is an entirely different circumstance, and likely immune to subtle techniques. Deep-seated resistance is not readily swayed. Through its sheer force and intensity, it demands to be addressed directly. The longer it is ignored, the more vehemently it will fester and finally explode. No, sooner rather than later, the presenter will need to directly acknowledge that she is aware of the resistance.

Here's the beauty of naming the resistance: the moment we name it, we're practicing one of the golden rules of conflict management. I learned this when I first became a mediator at the Brooklyn Courts. The moment something is named, it already diminishes in power. It no longer is this silent, unspoken force. Naming it is, in and of itself, a shifting technique. However, naming it alone will not release resistance. Now that we have named it, we need to work with it!

Here is the simplest and cleanest way to name the resistance: Take a pause. Survey the room. Make eye contact with your audience. Establish this eye contact with as many of your audience members as possible. And then open the door with a simple statement that holds up the mirror to what is going on. Describe what you see: "I look out, and I see a lot of slouching bodies and a lot of fidgeting hands in front of me. I also notice that there's a lot of silence in the room. Can you give me a sense of what's going on?"

You have just opened the door with this statement. You have opened it wide. Remember—your audience likely has very real reasons why it is resisting a presentation. In *Maslow on Management* (1998), the pioneering psychologist Abraham Maslow strongly urges every leader to "assume hostility to be reactive rather than character-based, i.e., that it will be for good, objective, present, here-now reasons and that it is therefore valuable rather than evil" (p. 27). If you are proposing a new business initiative, your audience may not believe that the initiative is feasible. It may be cynical because a similar initiative was introduced a year ago and it didn't work. It may be doubtful that you will provide the proper resources to support the initiative. It may not believe that the timeline for the initiative is remotely realistic. It may quite simply not believe that the initiative is important.

There are only two things you need to remember right now: Keep the door open wide for a while—you decide for how long. Listen, listen, listen. Then start to close it again—and you decide how far to close it. The conversation that transpires between the opening and the closing will let you know how to best proceed with this act of closing. Here are some pointers for navigating your "open-door approach":

• Be willing to hear absolutely anything that is said at this point, even if it does not fit in with your stated purpose for the presentation.

- Simply listen. Resist the temptation to engage in an instant debate with what is said.
- Show empathy whenever possible. Audiences long to be heard. The moment an audience feels that it has been heard, it will be a good deal more willing to hear what you want and need to say as well!
- If the audience is challenging you about specific details of your presentation, engage in a conversation about the points of contention. Note that at this moment, you have already shifted your audience from silent resistance to an active debate of the topic at hand. How wonderful!
- Your choice of question, at this stage of the conversation, will help to gently shape the direction of this exchange. Let us return to the just-mentioned example of a speech announcing a new business initiative, and your "open door" is revealing major resistance to this new policy. Here are some sample questions that are open and will at the same time steer the direction of the conversation:

  - "Why do you think we created this new initiative?"
  - "Why do you think the old initiatives were abandoned?"
  - "Are there any potential benefits to this new initiative?"
  - "What obstacles do you see for implementing this new initiative?"
  - "What can I do to support you in making this new policy work?"
  - "What can you do to help make this policy work?"

- The moment the audience engages with these questions, it is working with you and not fighting you. Moreover—these questions are beginning to move the conversation from a wide-open door to a more closed door.
- If you receive any new insights based on your audience's comments, acknowledge this at once: "I had not thought about it in this way before." "This is a very helpful perspective." "Your comment makes me look at this in a whole new way!" Your willingness to indicate that the audience has an impact on you will help to further melt any remaining blocks of resistance.

- If your audience asks you to follow up on the concerns it raised, agree to follow up. Make sure that you commit to the follow up, not to outcomes that you cannot promise at this point!
- Be upfront with your audience about what is negotiable and what isn't. It may not be able to hear this at the beginning of the dialogue you just had. But now, at the end, it will likely appreciate such clarity from you!
- If there are specific behaviors you need from your audience at this point—behaviors like "more participation" or "less distractions"—ask for them now! The beauty of the preceding process is that you likely will not have to ask for any of these behaviors—the audience is now already fully engaged with you!

As you follow some of the suggestions I have outlined, you will note that your presentation is no longer the presentation you had planned. It is, however, the presentation this particular audience needs. You have opened it up, and you have shaped it. Your willingness to engage with the realities of the moment will also have raised your profile and credibility in immeasurable ways. Audiences want and need to be heard; they don't want to be "talked down to." Chances are your audience will respect you, even if it does not agree with everything you had to say. Because of the way you conducted yourself, moment by moment, the audience will have responded to you—your essence, your personal qualities. Indeed, it will have connected with you without necessarily connecting with all of the content of your presentation. This is the core truth about all public speaking, and the foundation for every successful speaker, which we will explore with much more detail in part III.

PRACTICE EXERCISE

The best practice for engaging with a resistant audience is a good simulation. I encourage all speakers to prepare for a potentially resistant audience by conducting "a dry run," where they get to play out their worst possible scenario with an actual mock audience.

It's not enough to simply think about what we might do if "things don't go as planned." Every audience is different, and, in the end, there will always be a measure of instinct to our responses. So, to help you hone these instincts, bring in a sample audience. The beauty of such a simulation is that it not only helps you to sharpen your response mechanisms—any resistance that may manifest in an actual audience will likely seem like a mild breeze compared to what you had to address in your practice!

For this practice exercise, it will be helpful to gather a small audience of at least four to six participants. If you can rustle up eight to ten audience members, that will be even better. It is difficult to simulate the power of an entire group with only a couple of participants. To best practice ways of handling resistance, ask your sample audience to be available for a good half-hour or so. Group dynamics tend to take some time to build and unfold, and two or three minutes will not give you sufficient time to get a sense of the energy and life of a group.

Chances are your sample audience members will really enjoy playing the challenging audience for you. Most adults relish the chance to "be bad." Here are some guidelines that will assure that this will, indeed, be a useful practice opportunity for you:

- Clarify with your audience members before you begin your presentation just how resistant you want them to be. I like to discuss this on a scale from 1 to 3—1 being low resistance, 2 medium resistance, and 3 high resistance. If necessary, discuss with your sample audience what you understand as low, medium, and high resistance. Indicate to your audience the level of resistance that would be helpful to you for this practice.
- Let your audience know whether you need everyone to be resistant, or if you wish to practice working with only a smaller pocket of resistance within a larger group.
- Since this is a more involved role-play than previous skill practices, it may be helpful if you create a simple scenario for this exercise:
  - You might, for example, be the new CEO of a company; your audience consists of employees who have been with the

company since before you were brought aboard. You are here to announce cost-cutting measures!

- I urge you to dream up a scenario that will stimulate both you and your simulation audience, and that will feel "real" to everyone involved.
- If you are about to give a presentation at your actual job and anticipate a specific kind of resistance, consider role-playing this very real-life situation. Let your audience members know what sort of resistance you anticipate in your upcoming presentation. They can help you prepare by "acting out" that potential resistance in this practice.

- Give your audience a minute or so to strategize without you before you start this practice exercise.
- Be prepared to speak about the topic of your choice for about ten minutes. Make sure you know the topic well enough so you can focus entirely on how you shape and influence the relationship with this audience. Since it will be crucial for your audience to be fully present for this simulation, you may wish to set an alarm clock to help you manage the timing of this practice.
- Speak for ten minutes. No matter what your audience does, keep playing with different ways of engaging and re-engaging the group. Remember your two main strategies for managing audience resistance: You can shift it, or you can name it.
- When your ten minutes are up, stop—regardless of where you find yourself at that moment in the process with your group. Reflect first on what happened in this practice. Tell your audience what you believe you did well, and what you believe you could have handled differently.
- Invite your audience members to give you feedback. Encourage them to tell you what strategies they saw you put into action. Make sure they tell you how your strategies made them feel. A shift in resistance tends to happen in the emotional realm, and it will help you to get a sense of the emotional impact your actions had on your audience.

- Encourage your audience members to share any additional strategies, tools, or actions that you could have employed in the preceding practice to influence their resistance. What other words or actions might have lessened their resistance?
- Get ready for a second practice round. Make sure you use the same thematic content that you used in your first presentation. Let your audience know what new approaches you will experiment with in this next round!
- Speak for another ten minutes. Repeat the feedback process from the first round, with you offering an initial assessment first, followed by the feedback from your participants. Make sure you continue to focus on the emotional impact your approaches and interventions had on your audience!
- Invite your audience members to, once again, offer suggestions for other things you might have been able to say or do in this second round to sway their response to your presentation.
- As you contemplate your choices and actions in these two practice rounds, as well as the feedback you received from your audience, remember that this is strictly a laboratory process. There is no perfect strategy or universal recipe for handling a group, every time we encounter a bit of group resistance. There is no simple, magic answer. The more we practice in such laboratory settings, the more we will learn to trust our instincts "in the moment," during a real presentation. This is the primary purpose of a laboratory practice—to help you learn what approaches have a better chance of influencing a group, and to bring you ever closer to trusting your instinctual response.

The Art of the Flow

PART III

What gets across most is what we *are* rather than what we *teach*.
—Anonymous

I don't know who said this. I found this quote in a participant guide for a seminar that I was facilitating. This simple quote, I believe, is the one big truth about public speaking. It took me a long time to understand just how powerful a truth it really is. I feared it because it forced me to go to the core of who I am—that part of me I spend a great deal of time protecting and hiding from the public.

Ironically, it is also the truth that was hurled at me from the moment I began my studies as an actor three decades ago. Like many young students in an acting conservatory, I wanted to learn acting technique. I longed to master the art of sense memory and personalization. I sought to inhale the teachings of Stanislavsky and Grotowsky, two of the great theater gurus of the twentieth century, as if a feverish act of absorption might, by osmosis, make me a great actor. Instead, this is what Tony Abeson, one of my first acting coaches, asked of me: "Become an interesting person. Be curious about the world. Go to a museum. Meditate on nature. Read, read, read."

I yearned for technique. Tony challenged me to acquire the intangible qualities that color and inform any technique. This book, so far, has been primarily concerned with honing the craft and technique of a speaker. In this final section, we will take the plunge into our psyche and thought patterns. This is our very own, subterranean landscape that informs everything we do. Our conscious understanding of this landscape will be the single most important factor in unleashing our speaking power. It is here where we will toss out technique so that we may, indeed, master and transcend it.

I am writing these words a week after the passing of Katharine Hepburn, one of the most honored actresses of the twentieth century. In the glut of television profiles and tributes that bombarded the airwaves, one interview stands out in my mind. A neighbor and close friend in Ms. Hepburn's later years was asked what Katharine Hepburn thought of the more recent generation of actresses. "She really liked Sally Field," he said after a moment's hesitation. "Sally Field?" the interviewer repeated, incredulous and clearly more than a little surprised by this response. "Well, what did Ms. Hepburn think of Meryl Streep?" this interviewer persisted, as if trying to elicit a more exalted reply. Katharine's friend paused as if to carefully contemplate his answer, and then he said: "Well, Ms. Hepburn felt that Ms. Streep just worked a little too hard." And then, as if to temper his judgment, he added with a smile. "But I'm sure she would have felt differently about Ms. Streep's more recent work."

What this gentleman described, in a clear and succinct way, is the learning arc of a performer. Fresh out of school, armed with oodles of talent and lots and lots of craft, she hopefully evolves into the mature performer who has acquired a wealth of life lessons and is willing to let them seep into the work. She, to return to a phrase we coined earlier, learns to get out of her own way. As craft becomes internalized, effort fades and becomes invisible. The performer just sort of "breathes" her character. Performer and performance merge into an impenetrable whole.

A SPEAKER'S EVOLUTION

The arc to powerful speaking follows a similar trajectory. If technique remains just that—a bag of tricks and tools—and is not fully integrated into the way a speaker "is" in front of a group, the audience will always be a step removed from this speaker. It will sit back and observe a speaker at work. Technique, and the apparent use of technique, become the barrier. They will prevent the audience from surrendering to the presentation. So, you may ask yourself, how do I resolve this conundrum? How do I make this leap from technique and a bunch of skills to "just being"? Powerfully, compellingly *being in community* with my audience? Does this mean I have to wait my thirty years before I have the life experience that will magically color and shape how I speak in public?

First of all, here is the good news—and it harks back to the quote that launched this section: It's rarely about the content of what we are saying; it's about what we radiate from the inside. My clients like to fight me tooth and nail on this one. I hear it over and over: "What can I do—the content I have to deliver is so dry and boring!" And I empathize, to a point. Some presenters have to deliver content that few folks would describe as compelling or motivational. Delivering a talk about a life-changing personal event may, indeed, seem a good deal more riveting than a speech about complying with mandatory government safety regulations. But rest assured: I have witnessed speaker after speaker mangle an emotionally charged personal story, and I have witnessed many a presenter talk about safety procedures with eloquence and grace.

I learned this lesson, once and for all, when I first began delivering seminars for Langevin Learning Services, the preeminent train-the-trainer company in the world. Soon, I found myself facilitating eighteen different seminars for this company, and like every speaker, I have some topics that I prefer to others. My least favorite seminar, by far, was a two-day course on project management. I dreaded preparing for this seminar when it was first assigned to me. I procrastinated for as long as I could. I have managed projects, and on this I am very clear: I am not passionate about project management. I don't enjoy the administrative aspects of project management. I don't like multitasking. I am not terribly interested in motivating underperforming team members. Truth be told—I am resolutely averse to everything that is essential to being a good project manager.

It turned out to be one of my most successful seminars for Langevin Learning Services.

This seminar, in a way, became my very own public speaking teacher. Because I couldn't rely on my interest in the content I was presenting, I had to dig deep to find my reason for getting up and presenting this material (and this required digging beyond the incentive of the paycheck). I had to drill down to the core of who I was and what I valued. What gave me the right to get up and talk to these folks in the first place? If it wasn't the content, what was it that truly mattered to me when I spoke? Did I have another, underlying reason for speaking in public? What did I really value about this odd and magical act of communicating with an audience?

THE EVOLUTIONARY BLUEPRINT

In this third section, we will peek under the covers and give a little dusting to the personal subtext of a speaker. First, I will invite you to investigate your personal values—they are the secret reason why you get up to speak in front of a group. The core that remains constant, regardless of the topic of a particular presentation. We will explore ways of crystallizing these values and bringing them to conscious-ness. And then we will look at any blocks or barriers that keep this intent from ringing out in an unfettered way. Not the physical or vocal barriers—we looked at those in the first section of the book. No, we want to remove the psychological blocks that may prevent us from fully shining in public.

I liken what we do here to looking at a house. Many of us like the freshly painted house that looks flawless and immaculate. Pretty. And often impenetrable. I have always been more intrigued by the slightly tattered house that is a bit chipped and reveals a prior layer of paint. The colors beneath the surface color. The blueprint behind the veneer. The origin of the building, if you will. My dad was an architect, and I grew up studying the blue-prints of the buildings he was about to build. Even as a little boy

I understood that these blueprints were the foundation for a solid building. They were the tangible manifestation of a clear, specific vision of excellence. No matter how much anyone dressed up a house on the outside, if this blueprint was not soundly drawn and executed, the house would eventually crack and collapse.

So let us explore the blueprint of a public speaker. To help us with our exploration, I have synthesized this seemingly elusive human map into four specific principles. These four principles, and our relationship to each of them, comprise the core that we will investigate and polish. Our ability to engage in a dialogue with them will have a disproportionately powerful influence on our impact as speakers. Because I want to entice you toward action, I have phrased these four principles in terms of action language:

1. Clarify the personal values that shape every encounter you have
2. Release your fears
3. Embrace your spontaneity
4. Leap beyond the confines of your well-defined walls

Consider this section your *personal* homework. The assignments here are private explorations that you will need to conduct without the presence of others. The clarity you find in these explorations will lift your public speaking experience into a whole new realm—an exalted, more resonant, truly powerful zone. It will bring you closer to those magical moments of flow when everything you undertake seems to unfurl without effort. It will also help transform every relationship you engage in, every moment of your life. And this act of being in relationship—I hope this is clear by now—is the true secret of speaking to anyone.

CHAPTER 11

Clarifying Values

Visualize a guy named Bob. He showed up at a seminar I was conducting in Minneapolis-St. Paul. Bob swaggered into the meeting
room with the gruff, no-nonsense demeanor of a seasoned cow-
boy. Portly and hulking, he seemed to be the very embodiment of
a lifelong factory man. As it turned out, Bob had worked for Winnebago Mobile Homes for thirty-two years, almost since the very
day the company was founded. His job title was "Product Trainer,"
and that indeed was what he did. Bob went around the country to
get Winnebago sales reps excited about the latest product fea-
tures. He clearly knew his stuff and spoke about mobile homes
with terrific enthusiasm.

I enjoyed Bob a lot, as did the other participants in the seminar.
His passion for mobile homes, and his knowledge of the product,
were brilliantly evident. Bob was an almost iconic American speaker:
the fast-talking, charged-up salesman. Bob received a good deal of
very consistent feedback from his colleagues in the group, and it
went something like this: "Bob, smile a little more." "Bob, show us a
little more of your warm side." "Bob, relax a little."

Bob's disarming and also very-revealing answer was: "But I'm a
product guy."

Bob had placed himself squarely into "the content box." He
believed that the content he was communicating was the most

important part of his presentation. His audience members, down the line, focused on the personal qualities they wished to see in him. While Bob was busy hurling product information at the room, his audience longed for a gentler invitation. As I observed the feedback exchange between Bob and his audience, I realized I was witnessing a classic duel between the significance of content and the power of personal essence. Our goal, of course, is to create a beautiful fusion between these two elements. Fellow seminar participants longed for changes in the outer manifestation of Bob's speaking style, but it seemed to me that Bob's impact as a speaker would only shift with an *inner* adjustment. Bob clearly knew how to smile and be engaging. What he failed to understand was that the smile and warmth are signals that reveal a speaker's regard for an audience. His audience longed to feel this regard, not simply to know it—no, *feel* it, *sense* it, in a palpable way. Bob needed to discover a compelling reason beyond sharing product knowledge for standing up in front of a group.

Let's consider another speaker. Denise Shanklin is the sort of presenter who I consider a bona fide *star*. I don't use that term lightly—it's a label that is tossed about much too freely in the public speaking world. A star, to my mind, is that exceptional person who can engage any audience with effortless grace. Watching Denise present in public is like witnessing a love affair between the presenter and the audience. You know the sort of person who people describe by saying "There isn't a mean bone in her body?" That's Denise. She speaks with a luxurious, slow Texan drawl that is entirely disarming, and every pore of her being oozes warmth and graciousness. I have seen the most toughened seminar warriors melt in Denise's presence. When I asked Denise to share with me one tip about public speaking, she said: "Make every single person in the audience feel that you care."

Her answer was not about content. It was about a core belief that motivates her as a speaker. I have, of course, heard other speakers espouse comparable values—sometimes in front of large audiences who they are supposed to motivate to honor similar values.

More often than not, the manager who passes such corporate values onto his flock does not truly "live" them himself. Invariably, his words sound empty and hollow. Well, the moment Denise gave me her answer, it made sense. That indeed is what Denise embodies for her audiences. It is the secret of her success as a speaker. And it is not an empty value—no, it is at the center of how Denise relates to anyone. Regardless of the words that fall from her mouth, this is the essence that her audiences receive.

Stephen Covey, in his now-classic *The 7 Habits of Highly Successful People*, argues convincingly for the sort of paradigm alignment that may lift a speaker like Bob into the speaking realm of Denise. He distinguishes between the personality ethic, where leadership is fueled by a set of frequently slick and not always sincere quick-influence communication tricks, and the character ethic, which is anchored in a core of simple and universal principles. Principles, as defined by Covey, are guidelines for human behavior that have been proven across cultures and throughout time. Examples of such universal and timeless guidelines are the principles of excellence, service, fairness, patience, and compassion. The golden rule is a great example of a principle we all know. These are the sorts of principles that are tough to argue with. On a deep, gut level, they make sense: they describe the way most of us would like to be treated by others.

Values are a different matter. If principles—much like the initial drawings of the architect—are the universal blueprint, then values may be viewed as the personal translation of this blueprint. Sometimes translations are terrifically accurate. Translations, at their best, crystallize and clarify the original source. Frequently, however, they change and diminish the original text. At times, they willfully distort it. Terrorists who kill innocent people are motivated by clearly articulated values. Their values are hardly in tune with universal law. The more clearly our personal values align with timeless human law, the more likely it is that our essence will connect with our audience. Denise is clearly guided by values that consciously matter to her, and more powerfully, values that exist in universal alignment. Together, they make for a truly winning combination.

CONQUERING THE DIVIDE

In this chapter, I invite you to look at how you come across to your audiences. Where are your personal "inner disconnects?" Do your audiences "get" who you are, or is there a chasm between what you say and what you value? How fully do you embody your values? To what degree are your values in sync with what might unarguably be considered timeless universal principles? Public behavior is an unflinching magnifying glass for the inner rifts and imbalances we have worked so hard to hide. If we operate from an internal disconnect, it inevitably will show up the moment we speak in the public realm.

Back in the mid-nineties, I was dispatched to a New York City public school in Queens to conduct a little bit of organizational mediation. What I encountered there was a principal who was operating with a classic disconnect. The Board of Education had newly transferred him to run the school, and I had been told that there were big conflicts between the school staff and the principal. When I met the principal, I was startled by what a terrific communicator he was. Energetic and articulate, poised and charming, he was clearly in command of the sort of inclusive and bridge-building communication skills that leaders are taught these days. I was impressed by this guy, and he won me over quickly. But the moment I spoke to some of his staff members I had my lightbulb moment. They perceived him as slick. They felt manipulated by him. They certainly never believed that he cared about every single one of them—the Denise core value. I had stumbled onto a clear case of the well-packaged personality, and his school audience wasn't as gullible as I had been upon first meeting him. One of his core values likely was that "if I try hard enough, I'll win them over." He was trying, indeed. But his audience saw only effort without sincerity of intent. This gap between effort and intent made his every action appear hollow. More effort simply begot more distrust and resistance from his audience.

Sincerity—and a genuine way of showing interest in one's audience—is one of those core values that is essential for a speaker's success. It is also, cynics notwithstanding, impossible to fake sincerity over any length of time. I have had heated debates with clients from Great Britain and French-speaking Canada over this topic. Both client groups impressed on me that, in their cultures, sarcasm is a highly valued way of communicating with others. Instinctively, however, they seemed to know that sarcasm is not a relationship-builder with an audience, regardless of the cultural framework. When it was time for them to get up and speak in a workshop, every single one of these speakers who hotly raised the sarcasm issue chose a sincere speaking style.

In a public-speaking course I sometimes conduct a simple exercise in which participants are given a short line of dialogue. They deliver it twice—once sincerely, once sarcastically. It never ceases to amaze me how often the audience cannot tell whether it is listening to the sincere or the sarcastic interpretation. A speaker who believes he is speaking with sincerity but is perceived as sarcastic is operating with a major disconnect. A speaker who believes she is warm and inviting but is perceived as arrogant and aloof is operating with an inner gap. We can play and play with different ways of delivering a line (the technique level), but the same misperception will soon be re-created on another line. These disconnects can only be fixed by a conscious and committed value tune-up.

ILLUMINATING THE SUBTEXT

How do we conduct such a tune-up? How do we get to this wonderfully liberating place of it not always being about what we say but what we radiate? Let us begin by being conscious of what our values are. Let us name them and give them a voice. Let us make them the anchor for every moment when we speak to an audience, no matter how turbulent the currents in this particular harbor may be.

Many of us walk through life operating from unarticulated or semiconscious beliefs. Few speakers, for example, will say this to me directly, but when I conduct a workshop where we explore ways of working with a challenging group, this is what I hear between the lines: The audience is the enemy. Now that is a powerful belief. If I operate from this core belief, it will work against what I need to do as a presenter, every time. It will sabotage any possibility of shared enlightenment with a group. It will make it impossible to forge a bond with this audience. Would a core belief that all people long for meaning and connection not serve us better? No matter what the surface behavior of an audience—and there will be times when audience members exhibit hostility toward me or the event where I am featured—a belief such as "Well, this is just how audiences are" will do little to turn such hostility around. It will likely help to create or reinforce the negative currents in the room.

Twila Thompson, a partner at The Actors Institute in New York City, devotes a good chunk of her coaching time with a speaker on helping him to gain clarity about what drives and motivates him. Every client she coaches develops a written personal platform. "It is very powerful for clients when they hear their own point of view," Twila explains. "Many have never heard it! So I ask them to write down their vision of the world that informs everything they say in public. I let them know that I am hungry for their point of view." I concur—writing a personal platform is a truly remarkable way of claiming what we value and stand for! Whether we name it a "personal platform," a "personal mission statement," a "personal inventory," or, as I have phrased it, a "personal tune-up"—we are talking about the singularly powerful process of becoming conscious of that which often hovers beneath the surface of our awareness.

As a writer, I have great faith in the act of writing words down on paper. The moment I begin to write down a thought or a belief, I start to commit to the intent and energy of that belief. Much like an automobile tune-up, it behooves us to conduct such a writing tune-up at regular intervals in our lives. The clarity that comes with a tune-up allows us to find the surprising ways in which a speech relates to those things that truly matter to us. We may suddenly discover opportunities to select new words, analogies, or stories that clearly align with our stated values. Even if we do not have the latitude to alter the text of a speech we give, such is the beauty of conscious values: Our values will ring through loud and clear, whether we explicitly state them or not. They are the personal essence that our audience "gets," on the visceral level, beyond what we say and do.

Writing this book reminds me, again and again, of the wisdom of actor training. Actors learn that when they prepare a scene and study a character's lines, what tends to be more compelling than a character's text is invariably the subtext, or what is going on behind the words. Actors carefully explore and create a lively subtext that illuminates a text in surprising and unexpected ways. The difference between two versions of the same scene in an acting class is clearly never the text, for the text is the variable that does not change. What makes one take of a scene more compelling than another is always the subtext that is created by the performers.

In the assignment that accompanies this chapter, you will have the opportunity to investigate your own subtext. I invite you to conduct this assessment with unflinching honesty. The more rigorously honest you are with yourself, the more fruitful this exploration will be for you. It is your opportunity to uncover any values, or repeated behaviors, that do not serve you and your relationships. These are likely the values and behaviors that unknowingly inhibit a deeper connection with an audience. Remember—your audience will always respond to your subtext a lot more than to the words you speak!

PRACTICE EXERCISE

In this exercise, you will take a detailed look at the values that motivate you and shape your relationships with others. Some of these values may have been at the forefront of your consciousness for years. You may also stumble upon values that you know matter to you, but that you never fully articulated. Realize that your responses in this exercise will reflect your values as you perceive them today. A year ago, your responses would likely have been different. In the future, your responses will just as likely differ from your responses today. That is the beauty of conducting a values exercise—it gives us the chance to crystallize our personal values, and it offers direction for adapting values and beliefs for the future.

There are five stages to this exercise. To experience the true benefit of this activity, I strongly urge you to complete each section, in order, and not advance until you are satisfied that you have answered each step as honestly as you can.

Section I: Identify Your Values (Five to Ten Minutes)

Here's where you select the top ten values that define how you relate to others, and what is important to you in an exchange with another person or a group. You may select your values from the list of twenty-five values that I have listed for you, or you may wish to add others that are not on this list. This is about becoming conscious of values. Some of these values may already be clear to you. Others may be values that motivate you in certain situations, although you had never really thought about them. Those are the ones that are likely to yield especially interesting information.

A tip: Don't over-think this exercise. Go with your gut reactions, and do not take longer than ten minutes to come up with your top ten values.

Personal Values: Check the Values That Matter to You

❏ Competition
❏ Cooperation
❏ Enthusiasm
❏ Empathy
❏ Excitement
❏ Expressiveness
❏ Fairness
❏ Fun
❏ Honesty
❏ Harmony
❏ Humor
❏ Integrity
❏ Intuition
❏ Kindness
❏ Mutuality

- ❏ Order
- ❏ Participation
- ❏ Patience
- ❏ Rationality
- ❏ Recognition
- ❏ Risk-taking
- ❏ Sincerity
- ❏ Spontaneity
- ❏ Structure
- ❏ Wit
- ❏ Additional values

If you have checked more than ten personal values, revisit your responses and select the ten from your list that seem to be the most significant. If you have checked fewer than ten, don't worry—we will continue to explore further only those values that you have identified here.

Section II: Prioritize Your Values (Ten to Fifteen Minutes)

Now we will take a closer peek at your top ten values. Think of the many different interactions you have had with people over the last week. These may be interactions at home, in the workplace, or in a public space with strangers.

We will assess your actual relationship to these values in two different ways:

First, we will look at how frequently you have actually expressed this value in a tangible manner in your actions ("The Expression Scale"). For example, if kindness is one of your values, how often have you interacted with others, either through a specific action or the words you spoke, in a way that might unambiguously be seen and understood as kind?

In the second scale ("The Consciousness Scale"), we will look at how frequently during the week you have been aware of this value. Again, if kindness is one of your values, how often have you consciously chosen to behave in a kind manner, or consciously noted the kind behavior of another and connected it to this personal value of yours?

Expression Scale

In the last week, I have expressed this value in a tangible manner in my interactions with others:

	3	2	1	0
	Daily	A few times during the week	Maybe once or twice	Not at all
Value 1				
Value 2				
Value 3				
Value 4				
Value 5				
Value 6				
Value 7				
Value 8				
Value 9				
Value 10				

Consciousness Scale

In the last week, I have had a conscious awareness of this value, either in my behavior or as I observed the behavior of another person:

	3	2	1	0
	Daily	A few times during the week	Maybe once or twice	Not at all
Value 1				
Value 2				
Value 3				
Value 4				
Value 5				
Value 6				
Value 7				
Value 8				
Value 9				
Value 10				

Go ahead and add up both of the numerical scores for each of your ten values. This combined score will become your Priority Index (The highest possible score for your Priority Index: 6; the lowest possible score: 0).

Priority Index

	Priority Score
Value 1	
Value 2	
Value 3	
Value 4	
Value 5	
Value 6	
Value 7	
Value 8	
Value 9	
Value 10	

You will discover that some of your values have generated higher scores than others. The values that you express frequently during your life and, at the same time, experience in a conscious manner, likely have more power than those that may indeed sound lovely but are not expressed through your actions and do not enter your thought processes. Note your top five prioritized values. Mark them or circle them. These are the five values that we will explore in a little more detail in the two upcoming sections.

Section III: Actualizing Your Top Five Values (Ten to Fifteen Minutes)

You have identified the five values that seem most important to you as the backbone of your interactions with others. It is quite likely that these are not the only values of importance, but let us take a look at the specific things you do to actually express these top five values. And since these are the truly important ones, let us look at how you can express them on a daily basis.

So, in this section, I invite you to list three specific behaviors or actions that you can practice every day to assure that you act in accord with your values. These may be actions or behaviors that you already practice consistently, or you may discover additional behaviors or actions that you may wish to consistently integrate into your interactions with others.

Value 1: Three specific things I can do on a daily basis to practice this value in my interactions with others:
  I. _____
  II. _____
  III._____

Value 2: Three specific things I can do on a daily basis to practice this value in my interactions with others:
  I. _____
  II. _____
  III._____

Value 3: Three specific things I can do on a daily basis to practice this value in my interactions with others:
  I. _____
  II. _____
  III._____

Value 4: Three specific things I can do on a daily basis to practice this value in my interactions with others:
  I. _____
  II. _____
  III._____

Value 5: Three specific things I can do on a daily basis to practice this value in my interactions with others:
  I. _____
  II. _____
  III._____

You have just created a list of fifteen specific things you can do, on a daily basis, to ensure that your actions, indeed, reflect your personal values. How many of these actions are already a steady part of how you interact with others? How many new behaviors did you discover that may further align what you do with the core values that matter to you?

Section IV: Actualizing Your Top Values When You Speak in Public (Ten to Fifteen Minutes)

The focus of this book is on the things we do when we speak in public, and the personal essence we convey. So, let us now look at the same five values that you just explored, and identify the specific things you can do when you speak in front of an audience to help ensure that these values are, indeed, sensed by your audience. Some of the behaviors you list in this section may be identical to those you listed in section III, but others may be different and specific to the relationship that is created between a speaker and an audience.

Value 1: Three specific things I can do to demonstrate and practice this value when I speak in public:

I. _____

II. _____

III._____

Value 2: Three specific things I can do to demonstrate and practice this value when I speak in public:

I. _____

II. _____

III._____

Value 3: Three specific things I can do to demonstrate and practice this value when I speak in public:

I. _____

II. _____

III._____

Value 4: Three specific things I can do to demonstrate and practice this value when I speak in public:

I. _____

II. _____

III._____

Value 5: Three specific things I can do to demonstrate and practice this value when I speak in public:

I. _____

II. _____

III._____

Section V: Five Quintessential Questions (Ten Minutes)

Here's where we take a final look at the five values that you explored in sections III and IV. We will put each value under the microscope with the help of the following five quintessential questions. The purpose of these questions is simple and also infinitely powerful: Do these values truly serve you, and do they help you shape the kind of relationship you envision with your audience? Make sure you apply questions 1 and 2 to each of your five top values. questions 3, 4, and 5 summarize and build on the answers you gave to questions 1 and 2.

Question #1: Does this value truly represent what I consider a universal principle (i.e., if I act on this value consistently, it will positively impact my relationship with any audience)?

Question #2: Does this value, if acted on frequently or consistently, have a negative impact on my relationship with an audience? If so, am I willing to live with this negative impact?

Question #3: If there were one value that I could remove, which one would it be?

Question #4: If there were one value that I could add, which one would it be?

(You may wish to consider some of the values from the original list that didn't "make the cut," or you may choose to contemplate other values that have popped into your mind as you have conducted these exercises.)

Question #5: If I were to embrace this added value, what three behaviors might I practice on a daily basis to help put this value into action? How would these behaviors impact my relationship with an audience? Am I willing to experiment with these behaviors in my daily life?

To help keep this exercise simple, I have limited the last exploration to adding only one new value. Don't let this confine you. It can be fun and exciting to explore many additional ways of adding value-based behaviors to your interactions with others. Remember—values have true power if they are aligned with universal principles and are practiced consistently. They become woven into every moment, every encounter, every exchange with an individual or a group of people. They change what happens with an audience in surprising and magical ways.

Completion: Statement of Personal Principles

Now that you have investigated the personal values that influence the way you relate to others, take a moment to sit down and write a statement of personal principles. This statement of principles will be your guide for encounters with everyone you meet, and the backbone of every time you speak in public. Make this a narrative statement. Feel free to include any of the writing from the previous exercises, including the ways in which you will specifically act on your values—and have fun writing it!

Here is a sample statement of principles, written by Brooklyn artist Ellen MacDonald, that describes her guidelines for how she wishes to relate to others:

I try to apply the golden rule in all my dealings with others.

I do this not only because it is effective; it is estimable.

In concrete terms, I think of each person I am dealing with as a sacred being.

I treat all people with kindness and respect. I realize I do not know everything about even my closest friends and I have respect for what I do not know as well as what I do know about them. By kindness I mean that I am sincerely interested in them and I take a moment to show it by remembering a past conversation, a friend we have in common, or an event we shared.

I cherish honesty in my relationships, so even in simple situations I strive to be as honest as I can be without causing harm. In other words, if I want to have more of a conversation than I have time for, it is important to me to say so and to make another plan to talk.

Wherever I am, I try to be as fully and consciously present as I possibly can be. I care about the quality of my attention and the attention given to me, so I listen and in other ways try to be present with my full attention.

I learned these ways of relating from the women in my family. Kindness, respect, generosity, honesty, and being as fully present as possible helps to create the warmth and trust I value and is a great foundation for any relationship.

One tip about writing this statement: Give yourself a time limit of ten minutes or so, and then simply start to write without worrying about the perfect phrasing or formulation! Leave the critic and editor out of the room for these ten minutes! Trust that the homework you have done in the previous five sections has given you all the information you need to write this statement of principles. So—just let your instincts do the work now, and don't let your brain get in the way.

Once you have created this statement of principles, revisit it often. Change and refine it periodically as you gain new insights about how you relate to others, and how your behavior shapes the responses people give to you. Know that this declaration will become the invisible cornerstone of your inner core. It will be ever present, regardless of the topic you speak about, or the nature of a particular audience.

CHAPTER 12

Releasing Fear

Fear is a wonderful emotion. And, we sometimes forget, a justified and necessary one. When I cross a road and a car is racing toward me at great speed, I am facing a real danger. Chances are my body will manifest a sudden physical response. An adrenaline rush. A tightening in my chest. A shaking knee. Chances are, as well, my fear will cause me to take action and protect myself. Leap out of the way. Run for cover. Fear, in this case, is an immediate reaction to an external stimulus. It can, quite literally, save my life.

There is, of course, a whole other face of fear. This is the fear of things that have not yet happened. The things that might go wrong. It is the fear of anticipation and projection. Nothing in the present has happened that might induce this fear, but this element of fear has the power to produce equally visceral responses in my body. Sweat under the armpits. A knot in the stomach. A tight grip in the throat. A flushed cheek. It is a fear that will physically inhibit us and emotionally paralyze us. This is the mental-emotional dimension of fear.

Sally Fisher, a noted transformational coach and political activist, describes this psychological dimension of fear with great clarity in her book *Life Mastery* (1993): "Say the first time you ever spoke in public you were speaking about a controversial topic. You incurred the wrath of many audience members. You panicked and were so taken aback that during a question-and-answer session all you could do was defend yourself. Now you have been invited to speak about something that is particularly important to you, but you are sure that you are going to be attacked again and that your viewpoint will be unpopular. You begin to panic every time you think about making the speech. The fear follows you around day after day. No matter how much you tell yourself that that was then and this is now, the fear hangs on. The fear becomes so real that you actually believe that you will be unable to deliver the speech, and cancel the engagement." (*Life Mastery*, p. 152)

This speaker's fear is informed by a past experience that was not positive. All future speaking events are suddenly tainted by the projection of a repeat performance. The same projection mechanism can be activated even if I have never had a negative speaking experience myself. Maybe I sat in a seminar and watched an unprepared presenter struggle with an unruly audience. Maybe I have a colleague who likes to tell "war stories" of all that went wrong during a particularly challenging speaking event. Suddenly, I have convinced myself that this is what will happen the next time I have to speak.

At the root of this anxiety pattern lies a deep-rooted fear of people. All people. Anyone, really. And absolutely everyone. Many of us are quite adept at masking this fear. We do it by being witty. We do it by hogging the limelight. We do it by not listening to others. We do it by interrupting that which we do not wish to hear. We do it by trying everything possible to pretend the fear is not there.

I see this most vividly with my client who emphatically reassures me that he is a "people person." The more loudly he proclaims this fact, the more I suspect that I am in the presence of a meticulously masked people-fear. As I observe him, he will inevitably reveal this fear by the manner in which he relates to his audience. He will likely do everything possible to command, cajole, and control his audience with his subject-matter authority. He will cloak himself in the role of the expert, and the perceived power that comes with that role. He will try his utmost to squelch, banish, and demolish any trace of his own fear, and in the act of doing so, put terror into the hearts of his audience.

This ingrained fear of people is a tough nut to crack, because the moment I speak in public, I am inevitably brought face to face with people. Not only that, I am facing them in a truly vulnerable way.

I am standing up in front of a bunch of folks who are staring right at me. Sometimes they stare more expectantly, sometimes less so. That is not a natural or comfortable relationship for most of us. My fear is, quite literally, looking me straight in the face.

THE SYMPTOMS OF FEAR

How does this fear manifest itself? Well, it comes in many shades and gradations, but the bottom line is, it's *all* fear. Here are some of the names we can put on it:

- Fear of looking stupid
- Fear of making a mistake
- Fear of saying the wrong thing
- Fear of not knowing what to say
- Fear of forgetting something
- Fear of losing the audience
- Fear of losing control

These fears tend to strike at the core of how we maneuver through life. The act of speaking in public simply throws a magnifying glass on them. As Sally Fisher reminds us, it's easy for our mind to justify these fears. They will likely be reinforced throughout our many acts of public speaking. There will be speaking events that won't unfold as smashingly as others. Suddenly, we are storing more and more fear data in our memory banks. We are meticulously banking our fear of speaking, and with each deposit we are generating extravagantly high yields.

There is a third level of fear, and this is the fear that is truly tough to untangle. It is a chronic, historic fear that sits firmly and deeply rooted in our bodies. It is so familiar to us, and we have lived with it for so long, that we don't recognize it as fear anymore. It has become a seemingly essential part of who we are. You have probably witnessed it in the speaker with the permanently hunched shoulders, or the person with a finely etched frown on the forehead that never disappears. This fear has become a systemic physical wall. We live with it every day, and it doggedly prevents us from connecting with our audience in a brave and brilliant way.

I lived with such a third-level fear for years. One day, after many months of coaching me, my voice teacher, Joy McLean Bosfield, threw up her arms in frustration. "There is nothing else I can do with you right now," she declared. "Your jaws are way too tight, and they simply won't relax. It's your German upbringing!"

Joy sent me to a hypnotherapist. Once a week, for a stretch of two months, this gentleman taught me the gentle art of self-hypnosis, so that I could release the tension from my jaws. Both he and Joy rightly understood that my jaw muscles were quite capable of moving. What had them paralyzed was a deep-seated terror: my fear of speaking up. My fear of being heard. My fear of having my voice. This fear hailed back to the early days of my childhood, to a time before I was conscious of what fear was or how fear affected me. Fear had found a very comfortable home in my jaws. It had taken my jaws hostage. As an adult in his early twenties, I had entirely forgotten what it was like not to live with this fear.

These personal fears can truly spin into outer space when they come face to face with the fears of an audience. Suddenly, one person's anxiety has the power to trigger a collective fear-fest. I was recently facilitating a daylong seminar on creative presentation styles. A participant walked in forty-five minutes late, sat down for a minute, and then announced to the rest of my audience that she had to dash back out again to find the nearest Starbucks before she could function. I was enraged. What planet did she come from? How rude could she possibly be? I wanted nothing more than to wring her little neck.

Later in the morning, as we had the opportunity to have a private chat during a break, I discovered that she had been in New York for less than a month, was brand new in her job, did not function well in the morning, and had done very little public speaking in the past. It suddenly dawned on me: she was absolutely terrified about being at this seminar. Her fear had unleashed my fear that this seminar was rapidly going down the toilet. Together, we were speeding down the highway of fear, and we were breaking all the speed limits.

MODERATING THE FEAR FACTOR

What can you do about these fears? Well, I have polled some of my coaching colleagues to find out how they address the experience of fear. I appreciate the individual spin everyone has on this phenomenon, so each perspective offers a slightly different frame for this universal experience, and I trust that you will find the one that resonates most clearly with your own experience.

As a speaker, it is imperative that I remain conscious of what happens in my body when I speak. If I experience a lot of fear, I want to notice how my body expresses or copes with this fear. That may seem entirely self-evident, but most coaching simply consists of creating personal self-awareness as a starting point for new behavior. My colleague Janice O'Rourke, for example, describes her work with a vice president of a consulting firm in Europe. She was hired to help develop his public speaking skills. Janice quickly noted that her client had no awareness whatsoever of what happened inside of his body as he spoke. When she asked him to describe the sensations in his body, this highly articulate man was unable to put words to what he was experiencing. He experienced fear, but he could not name or locate this experience. His entire body was separated from the processes in his brain. Janice's first opportunity as a coach was not to practice the delivery of prepared business texts, but to painstakingly redirect him, over and over again, to tune into the experiences of his body.

Such self-awareness requires vulnerability, and in a competitive business environment, most of us get rewarded for being smart, not for being vulnerable. Our bodies will actually do everything possible to block vulnerability. And in this act of blocking vulnerability, we hold onto fear and don't allow it to simply move through and then leave the body: "Certain things happen physiologically when people get afraid," Clare Maxwell explains. "I have often seen my students physically holding themselves up off the ground when they are scared, fighting gravity with their whole musculature. Suddenly they have removed themselves from the support of the earth. Students can lock into rigid positions so quickly when their bodies are seized by fear. But our bodies are designed to be fluid and movable, so I use my hands to ground and move my students. I help them to experience fluidity as a powerful state of being." Our impulse to protect ourselves from fear actually locks fear into the body. By tensing and holding onto a rigid stance, we prevent our bodies from releasing fear from our muscles. We actually fight the natural wisdom of our bodies, which wants to free us from this state of anxiety and discomfort.

Whenever I have conducted seminars with my colleague Scott Eaton, a psychotherapist from San Francisco, we have touched on the experience of fear. Scott likes to use the image of a hoop of fire to describe what happens when we face fear. We can watch the hoop of fire and become paralyzed by it. We can obsess about it, entertain it, analyze it, or recoil from it. We can be dazzled by the spectacle of fire. We can certainly walk away from a situation that is ringed by a hoop of fire. Sometimes that may, indeed, be the smartest and safest course of action. But the most expanding alternative would be to fully feel fear in a situation and then move through that situation anyway. Hopefully, as we leap through the hoop of fire, we learn that we no longer need to fear it, and that the anticipation of fire far outweighed the experience of moving through it.

Sally Fisher describes in very simple words how she moves through her own hoops of fire: "I am afraid of many things. I am often afraid of people but I just acknowledge it and leave my shyness behind in favor of being in the world. I am afraid that I am unworthy of the work I do, but I keep doing it and hope for grace. I am afraid to love because I fear that my heart will be broken. But fear should not keep us from loving or living."

The purpose of this chapter is not to eradicate fear. I am always a bit concerned when I meet a speaker who professes to know no fear. I suspect she may be the sort of speaker Janice O'Rourke was coaching—a speaker who rigidly blocks the experience of fear in her body, and thus also blocks any vulnerable communication with her audience. Fear can be a powerful motivator. It can challenge us to do things we might otherwise not do. I invite you to be conscious of what happens to you when you are afraid. Know your

fear. Make it your friend. Don't deny it. And certainly don't camouflage it—it will show up anyway.

There are two parts to our personal exercise in this chapter.
First, we will become aware of what happens to us when we are
afraid. I have created a "Fear Meter" to help you take a specific
peek at how fear manifests in your body and in your mind. Afterward, I urge you to consider the possibility of moving through
those fears with self-awareness. I cannot ultimately help you with
the second part of this proposition. Like many other folks, you may
discover that there are some fears that you can release, and others
that you simply have to live with. Your choice, however, changes
the moment you face this crossroads: Instead of fighting fear or
ignoring it, you may be able to embrace it as an essential part of
who you are. And this open embrace will lessen the power the fear
has over you.

PRACTICE EXERCISE

Fear is the one emotion that prevents speakers from being as vibrant,
engaging, and alive as they might otherwise be. Fear diminishes us. It
makes us hide. Change begins the moment we become aware of that
which actually happens to us. I have thus created the Fear Meter to
assist you in taking a personal inventory of the very specific ways in
which fear shows up in you.

The Fear Meter asks you to look at two dimensions of fear. In
the first list, you will jot down all the little things that happen in
your body when you become afraid. In the second list, you will
note what happens in your mind. Both of these dimensions tend to
interact quite freely with each other, but for the purpose of iden-
tifying their specific manifestations, we will separate them in this
assessment.

In addition, I have created a scale where you can indicate the
severity of a specific fear symptom. There is always a matter of sub-
jectivity when we play with a scale, so I urge you to respond quickly

and go with your gut response. You will likely find that fear shows up in many different guises, but that not every manifestation equals the next in power and impact. And that, in and of itself, may prove to be interesting information.

I urge you to fill out the Fear Meter as honestly as you can, without judging your responses. The moment we judge a response, we interfere with the process of becoming self-aware and actually continue to perpetuate our fears. If you find it difficult to respond to the Fear Meter in a vacuum, outside of the context of an actual presentation, you may wish to use it as a guideline for observing yourself the next time you speak in public. Fill it out immediately after that presentation, and I trust you will be very much in tune with the ways in which fear showed up in your body and in your thoughts.

Fear Meter
I. The Body

Where in your body does fear show up? What happens to the part of your body where you experience fear? To what degree does this sensation usually occur?

Symptom in Body	Degree to Which I Experience This Symptom			
	Very High	High	Medium	Low
Example: A tightness in my throat		x		

II. *The Mind*

What kind of thoughts do I have when fear shows up? How strong and persistent are these thoughts when they usually occur?

Thought in my Mind	Intensity and Persistence of This Thought			
	Very High	High	Medium	Low
Example: I obsess about forgetting part of my text		x		

The beauty of the Fear Meter is that it makes us conscious of all the big and little ways in which fear shows up. Simply being conscious removes some of the sting of this emotion. I also like the connotation of a meter. A meter can be adjusted. Maybe you will be unable to totally oust a certain reaction to fear. But quite likely you will be able to turn the fear factor down a notch or two on the Fear Meter. And that, all by itself, will make a difference.

If you have stumbled onto thoughts or body pains that don't just show up when it is time to speak, you have likely discovered chronic behavior patterns that reach deeper than the anxieties of a speaking moment. To best address such chronic conditions, I urge you to seek the help of a qualified professional—a therapist, a body worker, or as I did, a hypnotist—who can give you the tools to release this chronic condition.

I hope that as you explore the personal ways of your fear, you will realize that you already do things to help minimize its impact. Maybe you like to meticulously prepare for a speech. Or you're in the habit of giving yourself a personal pep talk. You like to say a positive affirmation. You visualize the perfect presentation. You like to perform calisthenics. You close your eyes and take long, deep breaths. Whatever they are, know the things you do that serve you, and practice them consistently.

There may also be those survival strategies that don't serve you. I, for example, spent an entire run of a play having a swig of schnapps before each performance. That is not a recommended strategy for dealing with fear. I urge you to know those habits of yours that do not help alleviate your fears. Then you are free to decide whether you wish to further indulge in these habits, or if you want to experiment with another approach. A lot of the methods for reducing the impact of fear reside in the tools provided in part II. As you shift your focus from how you can best deliver a speech to being in a relationship with your audience, any reason for being afraid—real or imagined—is usually lifted from you. A real relationship with an audience, even a difficult one, almost single-handedly wills your fears away. You all of a sudden don't have time for fear: you're too busy engaging with the audience at hand.

CHAPTER 13

Choosing Spontaneity

Let us toy with a few elusive concepts. Spontaneity. Inspiration. Intuition. These can be slippery terms, hard to pin down. That is their very essence, and their beauty. It is also the reason why most public-speaking coaches avoid them altogether. But every one of us has a personal relationship with these concepts. I refer to them as concepts, but they are, of course, specific experiences that all of us have had at one time or another. They seem ephemeral because they happen so quickly. If we don't notice them, they pass by and evaporate. If we seize them, they are ripe with possibility.

Twila Thompson of The Actors Institute has a very succinct way of demystifying what occurs in the moment of intuition: "It's simple. You have already perceived something and your mind has not yet processed it. It's not scary—you can trust it. Part of you is just moving ahead of the other part." In a moment of intuition I have received a message—an inkling, a perception—that does not originate in my mind. If the impulses for my actions habitually originate in my mind, this can, indeed, be surprising or unsettling. So what if I suddenly allow for these unsettling moments of spontaneity? What if they happen in the midst of a carefully scripted speech? Will they throw me off-track? Will they take me on a perilous tangent? What if I follow my impulses? Will I lose my audience? I trust you realize that these questions take us right back to the projection games that our

minds like to play—the mental fears that are not based on external evidence.

I used the verb "allow" to describe our relationship to the spontaneous moment, because many of us will do everything we can to
make sure nothing spontaneous happens while we talk. We plan,
plan, plan. Planning is, indeed, essential for creating the possibility of
true impact. It gives us the illusion that we have a measure of control over what happens when we encounter our audience. All we
ever have, really, are the tools to respond to the things we cannot
control. The moment we begin to speak, we actually have the wondrous opportunity to toss our plans out the window. I don't wish to
imply that we should ignore our plans. On the contrary, trust that
the planning you have done was so successful that you don't need to
hold on to it anymore.

Let it go.

And revel in the moments that cannot be anticipated. We
cannot strategize spontaneity. We cannot work at it. We cannot
will it into existence. The more we try to force it, the more we
block it. Only faith in the moment-by-moment unfolding of the
experience with our audience will make room for the rewards of
spontaneity.

ABANDONING THE SCRIPT

There probably isn't a single one among us who is *not* afflicted by
spontaneity enemy #1: *perfectionism*. It is the most limiting of the
walls we erect to hide our fears. If we have just traces of it here and
there in our everyday lives, chances are they will magically
boomerang the moment we have to get up and speak. We aim for the
perfect delivery of a speech. We pride ourselves on not forgetting
anything. We diligently stick to the script. We make sure nothing
unforeseen gets in the way. "It all went exactly as planned." This
sentence puts terror into my heart. It speaks of a presentation in
which the delivery did not allow for any of the variables of the room
or the audience to interfere. The phrase is likely uttered by the very

presenter who complains about how bored he is with delivering the same content over and over.

A few years back, I was sitting in the audience during a preview performance of a Broadway revival of the play *A Lion in Winter*, starring Laurence Fishburne and Stockard Channing. A play of verbal sparring and witty repartee set in the thirteenth century, the performance was unfolding at a steady if somewhat uninspiring pace. It felt like a well rehearsed, but not necessarily lively, execution of an old warhorse of a play. Suddenly, in the middle of the final climactic scene, a cell phone began to ring in the audience. There was a notable bustle and hum as audience members reacted to this interruption. After four rings, the cell phone stopped. Thirty seconds later, the cell phone began to ring again. The bustle in the audience grew notably louder. For the first time during this performance, there was a sense of electric tension in the theater. The owner of the phone could be seen scurrying past a row of seated audience members toward an aisle. Mr. Fishburne paused for a second, clearly annoyed, and paused again. Then he turned to the audience and said: "Will someone please turn off the f-----g cell phone?"

The audience erupted into wild, appreciative applause. Stockard Channing tried to hide a chuckle but simply could not contain herself. Was this a moment of inspiration? Lunacy? Appropriate? Inappropriate? The golden rule in the theater is that you stick to the text and the staging. Mr. Fishburne violated this rule—big time. He acknowledged the elephant in the room. He responded to circumstances that could not be ignored. This moment, of course, is what I remember best about that particular performance. It was an act of audacity and risk-taking. It was the most alive moment in the entire performance.

Now, I do not propose all actors abandon their scripts to deliver a memorable performance. Nor do I encourage speakers to use profanity when an audience member annoys them. But there are lessons we can learn from performers. Performers who are bound by their text and carefully rehearsed stage movements know to let in stimuli from the audience. The noise. The rumblings. The coughs. The laugh. The never-before-heard laugh. The applause. The lack of applause. These are the external variables that keep a performance fresh and unique. For a performer who is attuned to noticing these stimuli, they will seep into every performance in sweet and unexpected ways. They will not change the words that are spoken, but they will immeasurably shape the texture and quality of each performance.

The beauty of public speaking is that it affords us more freedom to be spontaneous. We do not throw off another actor's line when we say something a little differently. We don't step out of a carefully focused spotlight when we go to a different part of the room. We have the option to freely respond to any comment an audience member tosses our way. How extraordinary! I propose we forge a mindset that longs to incorporate the unexpected, that isn't afraid of a tangent. That trusts that this tangent will somehow relate to the topic or theme of a speech. That understands that everything that happens in a public event can have a connection to our stated purpose for being there, even if we don't immediately know what that connection is. This is the sort of mindset that spots and seizes an opportunity, every time.

SEIZING THE MOMENT

If we're fortunate, circumstances force us to be spontaneous.

Once, during a three-day seminar, I was setting up for the second day of the program. I looked forward to seeing my clients again—they had been a jolly and engaged group. I was casually sitting in my seminar room, sipping my morning cup of coffee and munching on my egg sandwich, when I suddenly splattered food and drink all over my pants. There wasn't just a little stain here or there—my pants were a total mess. As I dashed to the restroom to clean up I realized that with my frantic running about, I was making things worse. The stain was smearing and soiling more of my pants. It was now 7:20 A.M., and the seminar was slated to start at 8:00.

There was no way I was going to look even remotely presentable by that time—and even though I knew that I could explain this mishap to my group, past experience has taught me that such overwhelming visual matters prove impossible for an audience to ignore. My sloppy, messy stains would pose a major distraction. On top of it, I felt uncomfortable.

In the midst of my mental despair, I had a truly radical thought: I could race down to the street, hail a cab, head downtown to my apartment, change clothes, and head right back up to my seminar room on Park Avenue. There were a lot of "ifs" in this proposition: This would only work if I got a cab right away. It would only work if the cab didn't get stuck in midtown Manhattan traffic. I would have to forsake greeting my clients as I always do, every morning. And there was absolutely no guarantee that I would be back on time.

I dashed past the receptionist's desk and asked her to inform my clients that I was taking care of an emergency. At 8:05, I raced back into the classroom, more than a little out of breath, my pants freshly changed. It was, of course, the best beginning of this seminar day that I had ever had. My absence had encouraged my clients to improvise—they had jokingly created a new overhead slide, announcing that one of them would be teaching that day. They relished this chance to tease me a bit. I used my mishap as a learning moment, and the story of what happened turned into a terrific teaching opportunity. And all of us were energized by this unexpected start to the day.

My first reaction had been sheer and utter panic. I had been viciously thrust out of my comfort zone. In the initial moment of panic, I rushed about like a madman. I was riding the wave of the adrenaline rush. You have probably been in the presence of a speaker whose entire speech feels like a mad dash to get to the end. The moment I stopped, the next right action presented itself to me. The willingness to be still was the key. My stillness allowed for the moment of spontaneity. It allowed me to wait. To notice. To receive the unexpected impulse, or the new piece of information.

MOVING INTO FLOW

Have you ever watched a speaker who suddenly decides to leave a prepared script? There is usually a quick little moment when you witness the speaker's decision. Amazing things happen in this little moment of spontaneity. Even if the speaker is very polished, you've probably been aware of her clutching her carefully prepared homework. Sometimes you see it quite literally in the way she latches onto her notes or the document from which she reads. You certainly hear it in the mechanical-sounding emphasis of key words, the meticulous yet detached phrasing, the carefully plotted pauses to elicit an expected audience response. Poised, polished—and lifeless.

The moment she leaves the script, the quality of her voice actually changes. It is supported by a different kind of breath, and the entire purpose for the speech has changed. Suddenly, you feel that she speaks from the heart. You sense the connection. You get that what she says is connected to what really matters to her. It is as if a prerecorded soap opera had suddenly been interrupted by a live announcement from one of the actors. This aside is invariably the most exciting part of her presentation.

The outcome of such spontaneity, at its best, is a delicious state of flow. In his insightful and illuminating book *Flow: The Psychology of Optimal Experience* (1990), the psychologist Mihalyi Csikszentmihalyi explores the many facets of the flow experience. He argues that a state of flow, where events seem to unfold with an almost transcendent measure of grace and ease, will only manifest when our abilities to act and stay aware come together:

> When all a person's relevant skills are needed to cope with the challenges of a situation, that person's attention is completely absorbed by the activity. There is no excess psychic energy left over to process any information but what the activity offers. All the attention is concentrated on the relevant stimuli.
>
> As a result, one of the most universal and distinctive features of optimal experience takes place: People become so involved in what they are doing that the activity becomes spontaneous, almost automatic; they stop being aware of themselves as separate from the actions they are performing. (p. 53)

In a state of flow, self-consciousness disappears. Our sense of time disappears, as well, or it becomes readily distorted. Hours pass, and yet we feel like we have been engaged in an activity for mere minutes. There is a reason why activities that many of us pursue during leisure time are so appealing: all sports, games, art, and other personal hobbies are the sort of activities that more often than not carry the participant into a state of flow. Sometimes we're fortunate, and we just sort of stumble into a moment of flow. But Csikszentmihalyi argues that the most enjoyable moments are not those moments when we merely lay back, relax, and do nothing. Optimal states are more likely to occur when we are stretched to the limit, when our focused efforts combined with a measure of skill lift us into the flow state. Optimal experience is something that we help to make happen!

In the act of public speaking, a conscious effort is exerted by the speaker, but the flow process truly unfolds as the speaker receives the energy that is returned by the audience. Flow is in good measure created by the constant feedback we receive to our actions, and our willingness to notice and integrate this feedback in our behavior. The speaker who abandoned her prepared script received signals that it might be wise, prudent, and possibly *essential* to depart from the script. This feedback was likely implicit in her audience's response, or lack of response, to the statements that preceded her moment of departure. The feedback was, just as likely, not received in any specific or tangible way. But the speaker's willingness to sense what was going on, to know this information in that inner place beyond her conscious thought, made possible her moment of intuition and departure.

On the other hand, the speaker who seeks to control every moment of her delivery likely has closed off the channels that can sense such unspoken feedback. Her fervent desire to micro-manage the unfolding of her presentation actively prevents her from experiencing a state of flow. This is one of the conundrums of the flow experience: The moment we stop trying so hard to control, we actually gain a sense of control we did not have before. Csikszentmihalyi explains it as follows: "The flow experience is typically described as involving a sense of control—or more precisely, as lacking the sense of worry about losing control that is typical in many situations of normal life" (*Flow*, p. 59). A sense of control becomes a wonderful by-product of our total engagement in an activity. It isn't a true sense of control—many optimal activities are high-risk activities where things can go wrong, people can get hurt, and there are real physical risks. But in flow we actually gleam the possibility of attaining control, something that eludes us the harder we strive for it as the goal.

Public speaking, at its best, has the power to transport both speaker and audience into a heightened state of engagement akin to what we experience in high-flow recreational activities. Consider this chapter a meditation on the wonders and gifts of the unconscious. I don't offer any easy answers about how you will achieve states of intuition, spontaneity, and flow. This is not a quick five-step approach to enlightened speaking. But I do know that your simple and conscious desire to allow for intuition, spontaneity, and surprise will be a great beginning. Welcome the unconscious and the wisdom it holds. In his book *Acting from the Ultimate Consciousness* (1998), master acting teacher Eric Morris beautifully describes the joys that await us once we open the door: "The unconscious is where intuition and inspiration reside. Pique the unconscious, and you open the doors to magic" (p. 55).

PRACTICE EXERCISE

How do we practice an experience that we really can't "make" happen? Many of us are at a loss as to how we generate those lovely moments of inspiration and spontaneity that lift us into the flow experience. Truth is, it's often easier to know what not to do—all the things that most certainly will get in the way of the possibility of flow. That's not a bad starting point. When we remove the roadblocks to spontaneous experience, we are halfway there: we are willing to let the unexpected occur. We concede that what can happen in a moment's time has the potential to surpass anything that we have meticulously planned.

All of us have, at one point or another in our lives, experienced moments of flow. Most of the time, such moments have seized us like a sudden undertow in a calm-looking ocean: Quickly. Unexpectedly. Frequently with great force. Occasionally with a sweet, subtle grace. In this exercise section, I invite you to reconnect with the wonderful gifts that you were handed in such moments. We will seek to remember and re-experience these moments of flow. And we will do it in two very distinct ways.

First, with the help of a guided meditation, you will travel back to one or several moments of flow that you have experienced in the past. Some of them may immediately leap to mind. Others may be moments that you have not remembered for many moons. Your body is a powerful storehouse of memories and associations, especially those sensations that it experienced at peak moments. With this meditation, we want to bring these body memories and sensations back to consciousness. Quite simply—we want to re-awaken your hunger and thirst for this state of flow and inspiration.

Afterward, you will create a time-specific action list for seeking out activities and specific circumstances that are likely to yield states of inspiration, intuition, and flow. As we create more and more opportunities for experiencing flow, we become open to what happens in such moments. We begin to create an environment that actually seeks and fosters spontaneity. We draw more and more of those "surprise experiences" to us. We, quite simply, become *willing*. And all of a sudden, such moments will start to pop up everywhere—and that includes the occasions when we speak in public. We simply cannot stop them anymore.

Part I: A Guided Meditation

If you have never enjoyed a guided meditation, please relax. There is no way to mess it up. The only way to mess it up is if you worry that you can mess it up. You can't. All you need is a quiet place where you will not be interrupted, and a comfortable position for your body. Some folks like to sit in their favorite chair. Others prefer lying on their bed, or on the floor. It doesn't matter. Make sure you're physically comfortable wherever you choose to conduct this meditation. One tip: It is usually helpful to keep the body open, without crossed arms or tucked-away body parts. Keeping the body open is the body's way of saying, "Hey, I'm open to whatever information will be revealed in this meditation. I'm willing to let it in."

Since I will not be personally present to talk you through this meditation, you may wish to record the words of this meditation on tape. Speak the words slowly so you don't feel rushed once you listen to it and actually experience the meditation. If you want to have a bit of fun with this recording, play your favorite piece of quiet, soothing music in the background as you speak. And, voilà—suddenly you have become your own coach for your personal and private meditation.

Close your eyes and let your body settle comfortably into the surface that is supporting it—the floor, the bed, the chair. Wiggle and adjust any body parts that may feel a little tense until you sense your body giving up some of its weight. When you are ready, bring your attention to your breath. Notice how it flows in and out of you—down into your stomach and groin, back out through your mouth and nose. Spend some moments just noticing this breath. As it flows in and out of you, this breath that is always there activates the cellular memory within your body. This is the memory of all that you have experienced and known. It resides within you at all times, ready and waiting to be called upon.

As you continue to breathe, keep your eyes closed but imagine that your inner eye can see a field of brilliant white light. See your entire body surrounded by this beautiful, brilliant light. This light is vibrant. It pulsates with energy. Notice how your entire being is bathed and soothed by this light that surrounds you. Luxuriate in the energy of this radiant light that is suddenly all around you and everywhere. Breathe and draw this energy into you with each breath.

While this light is everywhere and all around you, notice how a long hallway appears out of the light. While your eyes are still closed, see this hallway with your inner eye. See the walls of this hallway. See the floors. See the light in this hallway. And see the many doors that appear on both sides of the hallway.

In a moment, you will begin to walk down this long, long hallway that doesn't seem to have an end. This is the hallway to the moments of your past, when you experienced bursts of joyous spontaneity. Moments when you followed your instincts and gained wondrous new insights about the world. Moments when life seemed to unfold with great ease and certainty. When you seemed in complete harmony with the surroundings and the events into which you had been placed. These were the moments that unfolded so perfectly that all self-consciousness simply fell away. Some of these moments may have taken place many, many years ago. Some may have occurred only yesterday. The memory of each of those moments awaits you behind one of the many doors that line this long hallway.

As you begin to walk down this hallway, notice the many different doors on either side of the hall. You will soon find yourself drawn to one of these doors. Pause for a moment in front of this door. Know that behind it rests the memory of a moment from your past when you experienced a wondrous sense of spontaneity and flow. As you push this door open, you will find yourself back in that place and time.

Notice where you are. See the details of the surroundings—the colors and the shapes that are everywhere. Hear the sounds that reverberate through this place. And then see yourself in the midst of this place, engaged in your activity. See yourself as you were back then. What were you wearing? What did you look like on that particular day? Let all of the details of the physical surroundings bring you back to what it felt like to be engaged in your particular activity. What motions did your muscles perform in this act of complete engagement? What sensations did you experience in your body?

Where in your body did you have those sensations? How did you experience your personal energy? And what thoughts, if any, raced through your mind as you engaged in this moment? Continue to breathe into every part of your body, and just notice the thoughts, memories, and associations that come to you as you linger in this flow-state of your past.

When you feel that you have spent enough time behind this memory door, step back into the long hallway and close the door behind you. Pause for a moment, and let the memory of this experience fade away. As you continue to walk down the hallway, you will walk past more and more doors. Behind each door is another memory of a moment from your past—a moment when you experienced the delights of spontaneous action and flow. You will notice that some of these doors are left ajar. Whenever a door begins to call to you, stop and take a peek at the moment that awaits you behind the door. You may choose to simply take a quick peek at this moment, or you may step fully behind the door and revisit the moment in its entirety. Scan the place. Hear the sounds. See yourself in the moment, as you were back then. And remember the sensations, the energy, the motion of your body, the thoughts in your mind. The physical details of the place and surroundings will always bring you back to the experiences you had within.

Whenever you have completed a visit behind one door, continue your stroll down the hallway of your past. Peek behind as many doors as you wish. Stay for a while behind a door, or rest only for a brief moment to take in a snapshot of that experience.

When you are ready to return from this promenade, begin to direct your attention back to the brilliant white light that surrounds you. Notice that you are entirely bathed in a pool of this brilliant light and energy. It is all around you. It is within you. It is simply everywhere. Then start to bring your awareness back to your body. Continue to breathe deeply into your stomach and groin, and note the different parts of your body as they rest in their current position. How does your forehead feel right now? How does your back feel right now? How about your chest? Your buttocks? Your legs? Your toes?

Once you have completed this simple body-scan, continue to bring your attention back to your breath. Notice once more how it flows in and out of you. This breath has supported you throughout this meditation. It has supported you in all the moments that you visited behind the hallway doors. It is the source of all your energy and spontaneity. It is, indeed, the mastermind of the flow. And whenever you choose to do so, open your eyes and bring your attention fully back to the room in which you are.

When you are fully back in the room where you conducted your guided meditation, take out a notebook and jot down any impressions that stand out from this meditation. Write down anything at all that comes into your mind, whether it seems important or not. You may discover other doors, other memories that did not present themselves while you were in meditation. Notice what happens in your body as you make the notations in your book. The entire exercise was designed to help us reconnect with the experience of spontaneity and flow. And that experience invariably occurs in our bodies.

Part II: Action Plan

For the next six weeks, seek out activities that are likely to yield the moments of inspiration and flow that we have been investigating in this section. I suggest you keep this simple. Once a week, pursue an activity that has the potential to connect you more closely with the experiences of this chapter. Spontaneity, intuition, and flow frequently occur when we play a game, engage in a nature activity such as rock climbing, pursue an athletic activity, or undertake an arts and crafts project.

Especially with athletic activities, it is possible to be transported by simply being a member of the audience. The collective energy of an audience frequently provides a liberating release of pent-up emotion. In the arts, it is also possible to have a transformative experience as an audience member. However, since we want to relate our explorations to the dynamics of public speaking, I urge you to choose activities in which you actively exert effort. The experience of an effort that yields a moment of spontaneity will more closely resemble what happens to us while we speak in public, when we always exert a measure of effort until circumstances propel us into "the zone," when effort seems to totally disappear.

My Action Plan

• My activity for Week One:

• My activity for Week Two:

• My activity for Week Three:

• My activity for Week Four:

• My activity for Week Five:

• My activity for Week Six:

Please have fun with these explorations. Do not turn them into "hard work." The very reason I invite you to play with these activities is so you may rediscover this wonderful sense of full commitment and engagement, without it feeling like work. It may be beneficial, however, if after each week you take a couple of minutes to reflect on what happened for you during the moments of total engagement. What sensations occurred in your body when you were completely engaged in an activity? What did you do, or what did you not do, to make room for moments of spontaneity and surprise? What happens inside you when you shift into a state of flow? The more we remember, and the more we stay conscious, the more likely we will draw more such moments into everything we undertake. And that includes the potentially magical experience of speaking in public.

CHAPTER 14

Dismantling the Box

Here's a conversation I have every few months or so: A client rushes up to me with great excitement, describing a test that she has just taken to help her understand her personality type and how she relates to a colleague with a different personality. Usually, it's a test such as the Myers-Briggs Personality Type Indicator or another of the assessment tools that are popular in the human resources world. Taking such a test often provides profound personal insights for my clients. Suddenly, the sometimes baffling and unsettling interactions with other humans seem to make sense: "Wow, so this is what I'm really like. No wonder I don't get along with Joe or Nancy. . . ."

Used constructively, such tests offer tools to better help us manage the many challenging relationships in our lives—at home and in the workplace. Here's the trick, however: More often than not, my client views such a test outcome as the definitive explanation of who she really is. "No!" I want to scream. "No. This is a peek at who you are today. Better yet, this is who you *perceive* yourself to be today. It's a snapshot in time. I sure hope that one year, five years, ten years from now, some of your responses to the very same test will be a tad different."

Personality profiles generate deep, personal "aha" moments. They also create fixed and limiting views of ourselves, and our attachment to such test outcomes can become a barrier to our development as people—and as speakers. Day after day, we engage in a whole spectrum of adaptive behaviors that help us maneuver past the vicis-situdes of life. Many of these behaviors are survival mechanisms that we have piled on top of other survival mechanisms. We use these mechanisms to protect ourselves, to not be vulnerable, to hide our flaws, to banish our inadequacies, to not get hurt. They are the familiar ways in which we interact with the world. By the time we reach adulthood, we have amassed loads and loads of such survival behaviors. Some of them may serve us well, others not. They're part of the polished and impenetrable masks we wear to get us through life. They rarely are who we really are.

Why should we bother looking at this at all? Why does this matter to a public speaker? Well, somewhere behind the quick labels and the survival tools lurks the core of us that an audience "gets," in an entirely visceral way. This core is not readily labeled, boxed, or codified. Here, for example, is the most simplistic personality question (and a darn good one, too) that is consistently posed in the public speaking realm: So tell me, are you more of an introvert or an extrovert?

I, for one, shamelessly travel back and forth between those two domains of myself. As a child and as a teenager, I was shy, geeky, smart, but certainly not an extrovert. I was not emotionally expressive or overly dramatic in any way. No, the introvert label would have fit me to a T. Boy, am I glad no one ran a personality profile on me at that stage in my life and defined me as being *just* that, with the limiting view of myself that label would have bestowed on me. I have since learned to relish being in the spotlight. I enjoy the exchange of energy I have with my audience. I thrive on the nervous sense of anticipation that still grips me, every time, before I begin to work with a group. I actually appreciate the "tough" audience—the audience that wants to be shown, that has to be dazzled, and doesn't surrender to me right away. Yes, I both fear and crave those moments in which I have to fly without a net, when I won't succeed without taking a risk, and the risk requires that I go out on a limb with my audience. All of these moments tap into the extrovert inside of me— the person that grooves on the spontaneous exchange with another human being.

Which one of these sides is more of the "real me?" I'm no longer interested in neatly answering this question. I have learned, and continue to learn every day, about what it means to be comfortable with all of these aspects of myself. The beauty of public speaking is that it affords us an amazing chance to explore other roles, multiple personas—the many facets of who we are. It challenges us to step beyond any of the personal limits we may have set for ourselves, and the limiting views we may have about who we are.

Take Mary Boruch, for example. Recently promoted to the role of human resources supervisor at USCO, a company that specializes in warehousing and shipping services for an international clientele, Mary suddenly has to spend a good deal of time presenting in public. This is very different from her previous role as the company's librarian. No longer merely the thoughtful resource person that gets to huddle behind a computer and a desk, Mary now has to claim the limelight and inform and motivate hundreds of employees.

Mary is a self-proclaimed introvert, but during the several opportunities I had to work with her I was tickled by the vigor she brought to the demands of this new role. Instead of fighting the demands of public speaking or being paralyzed by a fear of failure, Mary uses her public-speaking responsibilities to explore previously dormant aspects of her self. I watched Mary experiment with revealing her sense of humor. I saw her play with her subtle sense of whimsy and drama. I watched her take personal risks by being a little flashy and extravagant. Instead of clinging to the role of Mary, the quiet librarian, Mary understood that she had the chance to uncover her extroverted side. And at no point in her presentations did Mary come across as inauthentic. No, she was simply connecting with a larger side of Mary that she had not previously revealed in public, or possibly to herself.

David Salvatore, the previously mentioned president of Blair Delmonico, has spent much of his professional life cultivating his extroverted side. His speaking style is quick, witty, eloquent, seemingly uncensored, and off-the-cuff. He projects the "in-your-face" energy of the speaker who you simply can't shut up. I was struck by

David's ability to chatter without end—it seemed at times impossible for anyone else to get a word in edgewise when David was "on."

Instincts told me, at once, that there likely was a shy and introspective side to David that he was withholding from the world. He paused when I mentioned this to him, and replied: "Yes, the pompoms are wearing thin." David realized that he was playing the role of the company cheerleader, and playing it all too well. The energy required to maintain this outer-directed role was tiring him. David's growth as a speaker clearly beckons him to embrace his introverted side. David needs to find the courage to once in awhile step out of the cheerleader role. Slow down while he speaks. Pause. Allow silence. By not fighting his shy side and integrating it into his public persona, David will become an even more compelling and commanding leader.

SUBVERTING YOUR CHARACTER

When I think of Mary and David, I think of an acting term that has become part of everyday language: doing something *out of character*. It takes a good deal of courage to do something out of character. The moment we act out of character is also the moment when we learn more about our true nature. In acting class, actors are often given the chance to play a role they would likely never get cast in "out in the real world." Actors do this to help expand their acting range. They get to play someone a lot older, a lot younger, a lot bigger, a lot smaller, a lot prettier. Fellow classmates get to witness an actor in the act of playing a character that's out of character for him. The actor, by "playing against type," is pushed up against the boundaries of who he is, or who he perceives himself to be. Acting class thus becomes a wondrous laboratory where actors get to explore different states of being. One reason performers get so hooked on performing is this extraordinary opportunity it offers to explore a character's full range, which is always a range and aspect of the self.

One of the worst comments a critic can make about an actor is that he doesn't have a range. Katharine Hepburn was slammed

early in her theater career in a now-infamous review by Dorothy
Parker, who stated that Miss Hepburn's emotions ran the gamut
from A to B. The moment we accept the underlying premise of
power speaking—that an audience really responds to who we are
and not what we say—it behooves us to explore who this person
is. We, too, need to find ways of expanding our personal range.
We, too, may wish to investigate the walls and boundaries of "our
character."

I invite you to explore what is unfamiliar to you. What is delicious fun. What frightens you. What seems utterly impossible. Know
what your proverbial personal box looks like. Then contemplate
what it might be like for you to dismantle that box. In a study he
conducted, Csikszentmihalyi asked a group of rock climbers, com-
posers, chess players, and dancers—all folks who consistently experience states of flow—to compare sixteen different activities to their
experience of being in a state of flow. This is the activity they
believed most closely resembled the flow-state: "Designing or discovering something new" (*Flow*, p. 256).

Every time I facilitate an international conflict-transformation
project, in which I work with individuals who come from countries
that are in conflict, I am pushed right up against my personal walls.
This is the work that single-handedly tosses me beyond my comfort
zones. I rely on the facilitation tools and skills I know (that's what
I'm hired to do), but every situation in this work teeters on the edge
of emotional chaos. Every project brings me face to face with all that
I don't know—about myself, and about the world. It, more than anything else I do, challenges me to consistently surrender my craft to
the instincts of the moment. I both fear and crave this work, just as
I both fear and crave knowing more about who I am. The lessons
I learn in this work are not readily packaged and bound, but I know
that they have seeped into every pore of my being. They certainly
show up every time I speak—in ways that I don't know about, and
don't need to.

My example tells of nudging my personal boundaries through the
work I do. It is certainly less risky to explore the unfamiliar when we

are offstage and not in front of an audience. The beauty of this is that it really doesn't matter when and where we explore. What we do off-stage will always inform what we do onstage. The moment we have tried something new and experienced something fresh, we have created a new body memory. We have new information about what we are able to do, new evidence about how we relate to the world. We have shattered a limiting perception of ourselves. How extraordinary! Another layer has been added to our character, or better yet, another layer of what was always there has been revealed. We just learned to step out of the way. Again.

SUBVERTING THE SPEAKER ROLE

These reflections lead me right back to the role we have dissected in the pages of this book—the role of the public speaker. Are you aware of what happens to you the moment you step into this role? Whether or not we view it as a role, our audiences will always cast us in it anyway. They make us the expert, the corporate henchman, the entertainer, the authority figure, the teacher they loathed, the parent they admired. A lot of major casting projections come into play the second we step up to speak. The role of the speaker can be an enchanting and liberating one. It can also be limiting.

We cannot control the casting projections of our audiences; at best, we can influence them through the manner in which we relate to them. But I urge you to take a peek at what you do, and the adjustments you make, when you inhabit the role of the presenter. I watch speaker after speaker who suddenly becomes a different person when he gets up to speak. The transformation can be expansive. The reticent person who has always been invisible suddenly sparkles and shines. More frequently, however, I watch the vivacious and engaging person turn into a speaking machine, void of the personal traits that I so enjoyed about him offstage. I quite literally see him don the cloak, the costume, the mannerisms, the very demeanor of the professional speaker. It's as if there is a specific mental imprint of what a speaker does, and it is this imprint that he re-creates. The person I so admire is swallowed up by this codified idea of the presenter. In the end, there is little left of the person I know: The schematic role of the presenter has become the limiting box.

Banish the presenter box forever! Toss it aside. Burn it and bury it. Instead, know that playing with the role of the speaker can be a lot of fun. It can become another part of the exploration of your personal boundaries and limits. I urge you to play with this role consciously. I urge you to make expanding choices. I urge you to do it with a sense of playfulness and investigation. Play with being a more formal, less formal presenter. Play with being more serious, more lighthearted. These are all aspects of your range as a speaker. But above all, be yourself as you speak. Your audience does not want to experience an imprint of a speaker. It wants to experience *you*. That is why you are speaking to this audience, not another speaker. You, and *who you are*, make the speaking difference. Don't deprive your audience of this difference. Let the brilliant essence of who you are sparkle and shine while you speak. That is the true gift every speaker offers an audience.

PRACTICE EXERCISE

I chose a somewhat bold title to frame this last chapter. And no, we certainly don't need to dismantle everything in our box in this exercise section. But I invite you to push the seams and edges of the walls just a bit. Much like we have done throughout the last third of the book, we will look at ways of clarifying what we already do, and contemplate ways of possibly doing a few things a little differently. Different behavior begets different results—it really is that simple. And the moment we let go of the idea that there is one best way of doing something, we discover a whole other range of powerfully being in the company of others.

I have a hunch you probably know the confines of your personal box—in life, and when you speak in public. I don't wish to arbitrarily separate what you do offstage from what you do when you are on. Public speaking is, indeed, a very powerful way

of being "in life." But for the purposes of our personal development and expansion, I invite you to create opportunities for
expanding in both the on- and offstage arenas. What we do in
one will invariably influence what we do in the other. Just as we
did in the preceding exercise section, we will create a list of simple actions that will give us the opportunity to stretch, explore,
and gain new tools and insights. Since the way you inhabit the
role of the public speaker is such a crucial backdrop to this
exploration, I will ask you to begin by taking a look at what happens to you—your essence, your being—when you step into the
role of the speaker.

Exercise #1: What Happens When I Become the Speaker

We will keep this reflection very simple. By that I do not wish to
imply that this is necessarily a simple process. But your insights,
I hope, will give you a good sense of what happens to you when it is
time to claim the speaker role.

I. Ways in which I "feel like myself" when I speak:

_____

_____

_____

_____

_____

_____

II. Ways in which I "don't feel like myself" when I speak:

_____

_____

_____

_____

_____

_____

Please note which of these two questions was the easier one to answer, and which yielded the longer list of responses. If you found these questions tough—because sometimes we're not entirely aware of what it is that actually happens to us when we speak—ask someone who knows you well and has watched you speak. Ask two or three people. What do they see when you come up to speak? Are you the sort of speaker who "turns it on?" Do you suddenly sparkle and radiate? Or are you the sort of speaker who starts to hide and withhold? Do your colleagues see the same personality they know from the workplace? Do they see more of it? Less of it? Do they see sides of you that maybe they had never seen before? Is there an invisible line that separates the speaker from the person they know?

I hope this simple reflection will help you gain a clearer insight into the confines you may, or may not, create for yourself when you get up to speak. The following two exercises ask you to come up with simple action items that will help expand the way you "do public speaking," and the way you "do life." Even though I separate these areas, the process will be entirely synergistic. An action in one area will always influence what you do in another.

Exercise #2: Five Actions to Expand the Speaker Box

Once, in the weeks preceding the December holidays, I found myself getting tired from too many hours spent talking to folks in public. There were those mornings when getting out of bed early to facilitate a seminar seemed near impossible. My body and my mind were tired. What I chose to toy with, every morning, was simple, and it did the trick in ways that I could not have possibly anticipated. On my short cab ride from downtown Manhattan to the seminar room in midtown where I meet my clients, I made the decision that I would have fun that day. This was not a fleeting thought. No, every morning, sitting in the back of a taxi, I made the decision anew that "Today, I will have fun with my clients." It was a conscious decision. I made it daily. And I tried to commit to it, to the best of my ability.

The results were delightful. My mental fatigue disappeared, and the physical fatigue somehow seemed less important. And I was able to remain open to the many spontaneous happenings that occur when we have a "fun consciousness." Those days of tiredness became a wonderful personal teacher. I have since continued to nudge my speaker box by much more consistently "making the fun decision" in the morning, and activating my fun consciousness.

This is an example of the sort of simple action that will likely have an exponentially bigger impact on how you claim the speaker role. Here is your opportunity to come up with five simple actions that will help expand your speaker box:

Speaker Action #1: _____

Speaker Action #2: _____

Speaker Action #3: _____

Speaker Action #4: _____

Speaker Action #5: _____

Exercise #3: Five Actions to Expand the Life Box

My friend Linda Carole Pierce is a great example of a commanding speaker: centered, kind, mature, and creative, she embodies many of the qualities that I admire and also aspire to in my own life. Just after her fiftieth birthday, Linda decided that she would finally learn how to swim, and she enrolled in swimming lessons at the university where she works. Now, that's a great example of an action that expands the life box. Can I prove that learning to swim will expand what Linda radiates in life? Well, I certainly saw how excited Linda was about taking this action in her personal life. I witnessed her enthusiasm and her firm commitment. And I have no doubt that the ripples of this accomplishment have already manifested in many other tangible and intangible ways.

So here is your opportunity to brazenly create five action items that will help nudge your life box:

Life Action #1: _____

Life Action #2: _____

Life Action #3: _____

Life Action #4: _____

Life Action #5: _____

The beauty of these actions is that you don't need to figure out how they will affect you or change you. Enjoy them and have faith. The results will show up in ways too numerous for us to list here, or too miniscule for us to understand. They will likely be intangible and invisible. But they will be there. Guaranteed.

Final Thoughts

I trust that by now there isn't a shred of doubt that the power of a power speaker is truly an inside job. If we want this power to have direction and impact, it is essential that we support it with a measure of skill. The kind of skill I appreciate most is the skill that has been integrated through repeated application, until it seems like, well, this is just how we have always spoken. Somehow the way we speak has imperceptibly and magically merged with the essence of who we are. Any trace of self-study, self-consciousness, or technique has fallen away. At its heart, the path to speaking power is always the path of tearing down the walls. As we remove our internal and external barriers, we suddenly allow the inner radiance that we all have inside to shamelessly leap forth.

It is my wish that, along the way, every one of us will be graced with many moments of inspiration. The tools offered in this book are the vessels that make such inspiration possible. Seeking inspiration without speaking skills is like attempting to fly a plane without a pilot license. All the fervent yearning for the experience of flight will not help me navigate the gadgets in the cockpit. I hope that within the pages of this book you have found a way to ponder and press the many buttons of your own speaking dashboard. I invite you to settle in. Enjoy the view from the pilot's seat. Remember that you have, indeed, been a student in pilot school. Buckle up, and release your fears to the awesome adventures of flight.

And the art in all of this? Well, I view it as the willingness to embrace technique and then let it go. To truly dance with an audience. To let the experience of speaking be fresh, every time. To trust the logic and intuition of each moment as it unfolds. To have the courage to surrender to an audience, again and again.

As I commit these words to paper, I remember a moment when accessing my own inner strength seemed as unlikely as the New York Yankees suddenly hiring me to play baseball. A few years ago, my younger brother committed suicide in a remote resort town in Spain, and my mom and dad asked me to speak on behalf of our family at his funeral. It was probably the toughest speech I have ever delivered, and every part of me wanted to run from this occasion. Yes, I wanted to take flight—and by "taking flight" I mean flee and not have to deliver this eulogy.

After a whirlwind of activity to arrange for such a sudden funeral, I got on a last-minute flight from New York to be present for my brother's burial in Germany. As I went to bed the night before, tired from the flight and the jet lag, emotionally drained from the jolt of my brother's passing, I tried to think of what I would say. My mind bounced and bounced about, unable to settle on any key points that I might wish to make in a eulogy. I felt helpless. There wasn't even a semblance of an outline in my brain. And I was afraid of delivering this eulogy in German. German is the language of my childhood, but English is the language I speak as an adult. I didn't trust that the right words would magically appear in German when it was my turn to speak. All I could do as I went to bed was pray for divine guidance. I woke up at about four in the morning. My torso and forehead were drenched with sweat, my chest was palpitating, my feet were numb, but I also felt a deep sense of calm in my heart. I still didn't have the words, but I had something a good deal more important. I had faith that the words would come.

I don't know what I said in the little chapel in front of my mom and dad and all of our family and friends. All I remember is that my mom came up to me afterward and told me how proud she was of what I had said. Somehow, at a time when I had been unable to plan an outline or write a speech, I had managed to summon the thoughts and sentences that needed to be said. I had gotten out of my own way. Delivering this eulogy forced me to practice everything I like to teach about speaking in public. It humbled me, once again, about the truth that lies at the heart of every act of speaking: It is always a simple act of surrender.

While I was putting the finishing touches on this book, I was sitting over a quiet dinner with my friend Liam Kiara in his apartment on the East Side of Manhattan. Liam is a seventy-three-year-old artist, former architect for one of the top architectural firms in New York, and a lifelong seeker of wisdom and insight. As we sipped our coffees he spoke to me about his relationship with the word *power*.

"When I was just a child," Liam explained, "at a very young age, I lost my sense of power. And my entire life has been a quest to reclaim it."

He paused, and then he elaborated:

"So every morning I sit down and write in my journal. I always begin by addressing myself as 'My darling powerful Liam. My passionate powerful Liam. My creative powerful Liam. My powerful true self.' And as I keep writing the word *power* down on paper, I begin to have a sensation of feeling powerful. I become aware that somehow, mysteriously, I am absorbing a sense of power into me. I begin to know, over and over again, what power feels like."

As I listened to Liam I understood that he was describing his very personal and private invocation of power. For Liam, affirmations are a clear and simple way of accessing the experience of personal power. They allow him to forge a direct relationship with this elusive and ephemeral experience. More importantly, he practices his invocation consistently. He has found a way of contacting his power with conscious intent. To my mind, such steady and conscious practice is the mark of a truly powerful person.

Affirmations are a popular practice that helps many people access personal power, but they are not the only way. I urge you to find a way that works for you. Most importantly, public speaking always involves getting up and actually "doing it." The body learns by doing and repetition. It learns the things that our limited minds cannot even begin to comprehend. So, I invite you to venture forth and apply the tools of this book. Go and do it. Speak in public whenever you can. Relish the opportunity to share your voice with the world. And, above all—have fun along the way!

The Seven Golden Rules of Visual Presenting

In this book, we have focused on *you*, the speaker, and the ways in which you access and communicate your inner power. I realize that you will frequently be asked to present in tandem with a visual medium: a series of PowerPoint slides, overhead projections, or if you are facilitating in a less-formal environment, prepared flip charts or flip charts that acquire content as you chart comments from your audience. Well-crafted and seamlessly integrated visuals have the potential to enhance your presentation in wonderful ways. Visuals that are neither well-conceived nor well-presented will always detract.

So here are seven golden rules to help you make the most of a visual presentation. These simple but essential guidelines invite you to be clear on how you position yourself in relation to your visuals, and how you navigate this potentially tricky partnership while you make your presentation. Managed well, this partnership will make your audience feel like it is witnessing a couple on a honeymoon cruise. If it is ill planned and executed, your audience is more likely to feel like it is watching a couple heading to divorce court.

RULE #1: CHOOSE YOUR VISUAL MEDIUM WITH CARE!

The medium of choice in many business environments is a PowerPoint presentation. It is an enticing visual medium that can add clarity and polish to any presentation. These days, however, most business audiences have been power-pointed into abject numbness. There isn't a week when I don't encounter a client who rolls her eyes and groans in dismay at the notion of sitting through another PowerPoint presentation. "Death by PowerPoint" has become an all-too-familiar slogan in many business environments. What was once a thrilling new communication tool has been battered into something akin to a ritual of public torture. A recent article in the *Wall Street Journal* confirmed this rising aversion to the PowerPoint lecture: While the majority of those polled affirmed their preference for a strong visual presentation, over 70 percent adamantly stated that PowerPoint was an overused medium in their companies.

I still believe that there is value in a well-crafted PowerPoint presentation. But know that you are likely tapping into this not-so-subtle emotional PowerPoint backlash the moment your first slide pops up. A few slides later, your audience will probably feel like they're being barraged by a stream of television commercials. Much as they do at home, your audience members will adjust accordingly: Get restless. Look for distractions. Tune out.

If you present in a formal environment, you will usually be mandated to use this medium, pitfalls and all. I will focus most of my tips in this section on ways of working effectively with PowerPoint. But if you have any leeway in choosing your visual complement, you may wish to consider an old-fashioned tool like the flip chart. Discarded in the nineties as a relic of the dark ages of public speaking, it is making a comeback as a viable professional presentation medium. Less formal and more homemade, it allows for simplicity and spontaneity. Think of it as the Mini Cooper of public speaking. Charmingly retro.

Full of upgrade potentials. Readily infused with your personal touches, it helps keep every presentation fresh and alive. Simply choosing a less-abused medium will send a message to your audience about you, the speaker: you have the desire to be adventurousness. You are willing to forego polish. You long to be less scripted and more "in the moment" with your group.

RULE #2: DECIDE WHO IS DRIVING THE PRESENTATION.

This is a simple but fundamental question I urge any speaker to answer: Who is driving your presentation? What is more important—the visual packaging or your presentation of the visual packaging? Are you narrating a tightly prepared script that has been largely re-created in your visuals, or are the visuals an occasional supplement to your verbal presentation?

I strongly advise you to place the visual in your service, rather than looking at this relationship the other way around. If you view yourself as essentially a narrator of slides, you could probably stay home and send in an audio recording of what you have planned to say. It would save your company a good deal of money. I don't mean to be flippant as I urge you to consider this removal of the speaker. But the moment I watch a presenter with a strongly visual accompaniment, I look for how this presenter manages the pace at which slides are hurled at the audience. I look for a presenter who builds and elaborates on the information on the slides. I look for the presenter's skill in personalizing the frequently "cool" information a slide offers. I look for the added-value information that only this presenter can provide.

Presenters send a lot of implicit messages to their audiences about how they view this relationship to the visual aspects of their presentation. The projection screen is usually placed at the center of the presentation area. Lights are dimmed in the hall to better see the visuals. The presenter is pushed off to the side, and sometimes not even properly lit. No wonder no one listens to the words this speaker utters. All of the visual elements conspire to make him obsolete.

It has become rare, but once in awhile I will walk into a conference room, preparing to conduct a seminar, and the hotel's audio-visual technician has placed the projection screen in the corner and a podium at the center of the stage. That's when I know I'm dealing with an "old-school" technician. His placement let's me know that he expects the speaker to drive this presentation. Now, I'm not proposing you banish every projection screen into a corner. But as you set up a room for a presentation, determine where you will place yourself in relationship to screens or flip charts. Decide on the level of lighting you will use as your visuals are up. Contemplate how much added-value information you plan to provide for each slide. Make a conscious choice about how you will manage this complex relationship—because otherwise, the relationship will manage you.

RULE #3: THE VISUAL ALWAYS WINS.

Quite simply, the moment a visual appears on a screen, the audience will focus on the visual rather than listen to what you, the speaker, is saying. The lure of a visual is that powerful. Even a poorly executed visual will yank focus away from you. If this were a contest between you and the visual, the visual would win. Every time.

So what can you do to make sure you're not competing with a visual? We use a technique called "Clearing the Visual." Simply put, we make sure our audience has plenty of time to absorb the content of a visual before we say anything that contradicts, elaborates, or deviates from the visual. Here are some common ways of clearing a visual:

- When you present a new slide or flip chart, step aside and allow your audience members a few seconds of silence to scan the visual and take in the content. When you sense that they have sufficiently perused the key information on the visual, they will be ready to give their focus back to you and listen to what you have to say.

- If you don't wish to indulge in these moments of silence, immediately give your audience a quick verbal walk-through of the visual. Resist the temptation to elaborate on key items as you provide this overview—your audience will likely be reading ahead and not listen to what you are saying, anyway.

- Elaborate on key items only after you have briefly given your audience the verbal "big picture" of this visual. Now they will be ready to hear what you have to say.

- Don't tell stories or anecdotes that have no relationship to the key points on your visual. Your audience will be torn—they will half listen to your story, half read the visual. They will retain very little of what you say or what they find on the visual. Make sure that everything you say is positioned as an elaboration of an item on the visual, or presented as an exception to information that is on the visual. Help your audience to connect the words you speak with the words or images they find in your visual medium.

- When you're done with a visual, get rid of it. Proceed to a blank slide or a textless flip-chart page. If you don't remove the visual, the audience will always be tempted to return to it. They will remain in a state of conflict between what you are saying and the images that are in front of them.

- Remember the "Taking Focus" exercise in chapter 2? This will be an especially powerful tool for you when you work with a visual. Move away from a visual to help give focus to the slide or flip chart. Take command of the space to wrestle focus away from a visual and bring it back to you. Choose and manage your focus with care!

RULE #4: DON'T UPSTAGE YOURSELF.

When you work with slides, it will often be tempting to turn your back to the audience and read from a slide. Don't. Know what's on the slide, glance at it if you need to, but stay focused on communicating with your audience. The more you read from the slide, the more you surrender your power to the slide. This is what actors like to call "upstaging." Instead of seizing a moment that is ours, we give it away to another actor. In this case, the visual medium is the other actor—and a ruthless actor at that.

To avoid incessant upstaging, we make sure we know the content of the slides as well as we possibly can. We relate to the slide content but continuously send our energy to the audience. This will also allow us to receive the energy that an audience sends back to us. A slide doesn't send energy back to us. A slide is the fixed, rigid part of our presentation. It doesn't feed our spirit. It doesn't surprise us. It adds nothing fresh to this presentation—only our audience will do that for us.

Some presenters like to use laser pointers to help focus the audience on key information on a slide. Laser pointers are a fun toy, but I urge you to use them sparingly. Like any toy, a laser pointer tends to draw attention to itself first rather than to the content you wish to highlight. It is not always easy to move a laser point with a steady hand, and shaky hand movements will be magnified as the laser dot does its dance on the screen. Fun? Yes. But suddenly—oops—you will find that you have upstaged yourself again!

RULE #5: DON'T OVERLOAD YOUR VISUALS WITH CONTENT.

As you create your slides, it will be tempting to transpose your entire lecture onto the screen. I strongly advise you to resist this temptation. Bullet points, key tidbits of information, and thematic highlights will do. Content overload will be an immediate turn-off to your audience. Too much information on a slide becomes an instant visual and psychological deterrent. When we engage in personal reading or self-study, we decide when we have reached the point when we cannot take in any more information. We close the book. We take a break. In a visual lecture, unless the presenter paces the sequence of slides and the volume of information, the audience members will also take their break. They simply will not announce it to you. They will sit there, buttocks in their seats, heads nodding. But as slide by slide continues to wash over them, they will have long ago tuned out.

We help our audiences by breaking information into bite-size chunks. As we create our slides, we vigilantly monitor the bits of content we place on the individual slide. Think of each slide as an appetizer in a multicourse meal: Sparsely presented. Delicately seasoned. Easily digestible. Just enough texture and substance to awaken the taste buds. And not too heavy to spoil the rest of the appetite. As you start to trust that it really is OK to present a little less, you buy yourself a good measure of your audience's goodwill. You will actually have the time to stay with each morsel of information a little longer, to linger and truly savor the information. How much sweeter this is than force-feeding your audience with too much content that it cannot possibly retain!

RULE #6: EASY DOES IT WITH THE SPECIAL EFFECTS!

The moment we embrace a visual presentation style, it is tempting to cross the line from presenting to entertaining. Technology allows us to create some marvelous special effects on our slides. Graphics can pop up and fly in and out. Characters can be animated. Music can add subtle emotional resonance or whip the audience into an adrenaline frenzy. And entertaining an audience is a wonderful thing, really. Most of us like to be entertained. We will be grateful to you for presenting a highly entertaining slide show. We will clamor to invite you back for the next slide show. But will we remember the content you presented?

These questions bring us right back to how we define the relationship between us, the presenters, and the technology we put into our service. The more fanciful we become with our visual choices, the more likely it is that the visual production will overpower our content. As you create your slides and contemplate the technical options at your disposal, consider the following guidelines: Will my visual choices help clarify a point I wish to make?

Will they help the audience remember this point? Will they help create an emotional connection between my message and the audience? Or will my visuals draw undue attention to themselves and away from the content I seek to communicate?

You will also have to make choices about the way you use color, and the amount of color you feature in your slides. Color can be used to create focus, shape meaning, connect concepts, and achieve balance in a visual. Research also indicates that most viewers prefer color to a standard white background with black lettering. Warm colors like red, orange, and yellow are terrific for drawing an audience's attention. They seem to bounce and jump off the screen. Cooler colors such as green, blue, or violet tend to be great for larger background surfaces.

Not only do colors have the power to evoke strong emotions, they also send indirect messages about you and your personality to your audience, so you may wish to consider your choice of color with care. Red, for example, tends to evoke and communicate passion, excitement, anger, intensity, and power. A dark blue, on the other hand, is likely to soothe and relax. It tends to indicate maturity to your audience and evoke trust. Marketing professionals make savvy use of the subtle powers of color. If you have to create presentation slides on a regular basis, you may wish to study color principles; you will likely find this research to be both fun and thought-provoking. As with the use of special effects, "easy does it" is a sound guideline when making color selections. It is rarely necessary to have more than three colors on a slide. As we force more colors onto a slide, we also force our audience to put proportionately more effort into decoding the visual and deciphering its meaning.

RULE #7: TECHNOLOGY WILL FAIL!

Be prepared.

Professional speakers love to share war stories with each other. The ones they tell with almost vitriolic glee usually describe a moment when a whole technical system came crashing down. Suddenly, an entire prepared lecture flies out the window. Know that this will happen at some point or another when you present with visuals. Have a backup plan in place. Some presenters carry handout versions of their slides with them. Some like to improvise and create flip charts as they continue to present. Others like to use the moment as a welcome opportunity to break free of the constraints of a carefully packaged slide show; they seize the opportunity to truly "own" the content in a whole new way.

Such moments of breakdown can, indeed, become moments of tremendous opportunity. "As a teacher, I have come to believe that many truly great classes teeter on the very edge of chaos," Stephen Covey says in *The 7 Habits of Highly Effective People.* The first time technology fails you, there's a good chance that it will seem like a descent into utter chaos. Know that your audience will likely not miss the visuals nearly as much as you will. They will, however, watch closely to see how you handle such a mishap. Respond with grace, proceed as if the visuals were only a supplement to what you do (remember who is driving this presentation, anyway), and chances are this will be your most successful presentation ever.

A moment of adversity has the wonderful potential to turn your audience into a stronger ally than it was before the incident occurred. It tends to activate a deep need many of us have to be of help and root for the underdog. For you, the speaker, the incident will bear added gifts: It will remind you of your own underlying reasons for speaking in public—the reasons that we explored in part III of this book. Most likely, narrating a slide show is not one of the core values that motivates you when you speak. A visual slide has certainly never been a universal guiding principle required for successful speaking—of this I am sure!

Sources

Barker, Clive — *Theatre Games*, Methuen Drama, London, 1977

Bolman, Lee G. and Deal, Terrence E. — *Reframing Organizations*, Jossey-Bass, San Francisco, 1997

Brook, Peter — *The Empty Space*, Avon Books, New York, 1968

Covey, Stephen R. — *The 7 Habits of Highly Effective People*, Fireside, New York, 1989

Csikszentmihalyi, Mihalyi — *Flow: The Psychology of Optimal Experience*, HarperCollins, New York, 1990

Edelman, Joel and Crain, Mary Beth — *The Tao of Negotiation*, HarperBusiness, New York, 1993

Fisher, Sally — *Life Mastery*, Crown Publishers, New York, 1993

Gardner, Howard — *Changing Minds*, Harvard Business School Press, Boston, 2004

Goleman, Daniel, Boyatzis, Richard, and McKee, Annie — *Primal Leadership*, Harvard Business School Press, Boston, 2002

Hagen, Uta   *Respect for Acting*, MacMillan Publishing, New York, 1973

Langevin Learning   *Humor in Training Course Manual*, Langevin
Services   Learning Services, Ottawa, 2003

Maslow, Abraham H.   *Maslow on Management*, Wiley & Sons, New York 1998

Morris, Eric   *Acting from the Ultimate Consciousness*, Ermor Enterprises. Los Angeles, 1988

Stanislavski,   *Building a Character*, Theatre Arts Books,
Constantin   New York, 1977

Stanislavski,   *An Actor's Handbook*, Theatre Arts Books,
Constantin   New York, 1963

Williamson,   *A Return to Love*, HarperCollins, New York,
Marianne   1992

Index

About the Author

ACHIM NOWAK is the founder and president of Influens, an international training and consulting firm that develops visionary leaders. Mr. Nowak has coached presenters from many of the world's Fortune 500 companies. His approach to the development of speakers has been honed through years of training actors and nonactors alike, for institutions such as the Kennedy Center for the Performing Arts, The Actors Institute, and the OBIE-award winning Theatre for a New Audience. At Influens, Mr. Nowak integrates his extensive background in personal transformation techniques, conflict resolution, and actor training to develop truly vibrant, authentic, and visionary leaders.

As a senior course leader for Langevin Learning Services, the largest train-the-trainer company in the world, Mr. Nowak has had the opportunity to conduct seminars about every facet of human performance improvement throughout North America and Europe. When not coaching business leaders, Mr. Nowak can be found leading conflict transformation initiatives in some of the chronic conflict regions of the world. Under the auspices of UNESCO, Seeds of Peace, NCCJ, the International YMCA, and the Peres Center for Peace, Nowak has spent nearly a decade facilitating dialogues across enemy lines. This work has taken him to Cyprus, the Balkans, and every part of the Middle East.

Mr. Nowak holds an M.A. from New York University in Organizational Psychology and International Relations and received his mediation training at the New York Courts. Since 1996, he has served on the faculty of New York University and has been a frequent guest speaker at other universities such as Amherst College, Brandeis University, and Columbia University. Mr. Nowak and his work have been featured on *60 Minutes, The Today Show*, NPR, and in the award-winning documentary *The Last Enemy*.

Mr. Nowak lives in Hollywood, Florida and New York City.

Do you have a question or an inquiry?
Please contact Mr. Nowak at Influens:

Speak with power. Change the world.
Training. Coaching. Keynote Addresses.
www.influens.com

 **Books from Allworth Press**

Allworth Press is an imprint of Allworth Communications, Inc. Selected titles are listed below.

NetSlaves® 2.0: Tales of "Surviving" the Great Tech Gold Rush
by Bill Lessard and Steve Baldwin (paperback, 6 × 9, 224 pages, $19.95)

Citizen Brand: 10 Commandments for Transforming Brands in a Consumer Democracy
by Marc Gobé (hardcover, 5¹/₂ × 8¹/₂ , 288 pages, 46 b&w illus., $24.95)

Emotional Branding: The New Paradigm for Connecting Brands to People
by Marc Gobé (hardcover, 6¹/₄ × 9¹/₄ , 352 pages, 134 b&w illus., $24.95)

The Entrepreneurial Age: Awakening the Spirit of Enterprise in People, Companies and Countries
by Larry C. Farrell (hardcover, 6¹/₄ × 9¹/₄ , 352 pages, 17 figures, $24.95)

Dead Ahead: The Web Dilemma and the New Rules of Business
by Laurie Windham with Jon Samsel (hardcover, 6¹/₄ × 9¹/₄ , 256 pages, 14 b&w figures, $24.95)

The Soul of the New Consumer: The Attitudes, Behaviors, and Preferences of e-Customers
by Laurie Windham with Ken Orton (hardcover, 6¹/₄ × 9¹/₄ , 320 pages, 59 figures, $24.95)

The Trademark Guide: A Friendly Handbook for Protecting & Profiting from Trademarks, Second Edition
by Lee Wilson (paperback, 6 × 9, 256 pages, $19.95)

The Copyright Guide: A Friendly Handbook for Protecting & Profiting from Copyrights, Third Edition
by Lee Wilson (paperback, 6 × 9, 256 pages, $19.95)

Please write to request our free catalog. To order by credit card, call 1-800-491-2808 or send a check or money order to Allworth Press, 10 East 23rd Street, Suite 510, New York, NY 10010. Include $5 for shipping and handling for the first book ordered and $1 for each additional book. Ten dollars plus $1 for each additional book if ordering from Canada. New York State residents must add sales tax.

To see our complete catalog on the World Wide Web, or to order online, you can find us at
www.allworth.com.